OXFORD MEDICAL PUBLICATIONS

Medical Ethics and Economics
in Health Care

MEDICAL ETHICS AND ECONOMICS IN HEALTH CARE

EDITED BY

GAVIN MOONEY

*University of Copenhagen and
University of Aberdeen*

and

ALISTAIR McGUIRE

*Socio-Legal Studies Centre, Oxford and
Pembroke College, Oxford
(Formerly University of Aberdeen)*

OXFORD NEW YORK TOKYO
OXFORD UNIVERSITY PRESS
1988

Oxford University Press, Walton Street, Oxford OX2 6DP
Oxford   New York   Toronto
Delhi   Bombay   Calcutta   Madras   Karachi
Petaling Jaya   Singapore   Hong Kong   Tokyo
Nairobi   Dar es Salaam   Cape Town
Melbourne   Auckland
and associated companies in
Beirut   Berlin   Ibadan   Nicosia

Oxford is a trade mark of Oxford University Press

Published in the United States
by Oxford University Press, New York

British Library Cataloguing in Publication Data
Medical ethics and economics in health care.
— (Oxford medical publications).
1. Health services administration —
Moral and ethical aspects
I. Mooney, Gavin   II. McGuire, Alistair
174.2   RA394
ISBN 0-19-261672-2

Library of Congress Cataloging in Publication Data
Medical ethics and economics in health care.
(Oxford medical publications)
Based on a symposium held at Lisse in the
Netherlands in Sept. 1986.
Includes bibliographies and index.
1. Medical economics—Moral and ethical aspects—
Congresses.   2. Medical care—Cost effectiveness—
Congresses.   3. Resource allocation—Moral and
ethical aspects—Congresses.   4. Medical ethics—
Congresses. I. Mooney, Gavin H.   II. McGuire,
Alistair.   III. Series. [DNLM: 1. Delivery of
Health Care—economics—congresses.   2. Economics,
Medical—congresses.   3. Ethics, Medical—congresses.
W 58 M489 1986]
RA410.A2M44   1988   174'.26   87-24747
ISBN 0-19-261672-2

Typeset by Spire Print Services, Limited
Salisbury, Wiltshire

Printed in Great Britain
at the University Printing House, Oxford,
by David Stanford
Printer to the University

Preface

For some time we have been attempting to apply the concepts and techniques of economic analysis to health care. For various reasons such application is difficult. 'Health care' seems often to be rather different from other goods and services. Certainly the markets in which it is provided tend not to be like the markets for most other commodities.

What is particularly interesting to us as economists is that the normal economic concepts of supply and demand seem to operate rather differently in health care. Indeed the demands of consumers (patients) play very much a secondary role and the supply side, especially in the shape of the medical doctor, tends to dominate. In such circumstances it is more than ever important to protect the patient through codes of medical ethics.

Yet from our (economists') perspective, there appear to be some tensions between the ethics of medicine and the principles of economics. To try to cast light on these possible tensions and indeed to explore more generally some of the ethical issues in resource allocation in health care we organized, together with our Dutch colleagues Henk ten Have and Frans Rutten, a small international and interdisciplinary workshop at Lisse in The Netherlands in September 1986. The papers in this volume are slightly revised versions of those presented at that meeting.

A word of explanation about the process behind the writing of the papers may be helpful to the reader. The Mooney and McGuire paper was written first, followed by the ten Have paper which is in part a response to our paper. These two papers were then sent to the other authors who were asked to write on specific topics selected by the four organizers. In this way an effort was made to obtain a structured set of readings on an explicit theme.

We would like to thank all those who participated in the workshop and in particular those who acted as discussants to the papers. (A list of the names of the discussants is presented in the Appendix.) Especially, however, we would like to thank all those whose papers appear in this volume. The meeting was for us a very enjoyable experience and the task of editing this volume was made so much easier than it might have been because of the ready co-operation of all the authors. An extra word of thanks is due to Manny Eppel who so ably chaired the workshop with the assistance of Frans Rutten.

Additionally a number of people merit our thanks. First, financial support was provided by the Dutch Health Council, the Dutch Ministry of

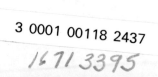

Health, and the University of Aberdeen's Health Economics Research Unit. Second, to our fellow organizers, Frans and Henk, we are most indebted. Third, we wish to thank Isabel Tudhope and Rochelle Coutts for their assistance in organizing materials for the workshop. Finally, thanks to Anne and tak til Anita, Rikke og Johannes, for their patience and encouragement.

Copenhagen   G. H. M.
Aberdeen   A. McG.
December 1986

Contents

5. Economics, ethics, law, and medical conduct 56

H. D. C. ROSCAM ABBING

6. Financing of medical services and medical ethics 73

P. SOHL

7. Medical ethics and economics in clinical decision making 90

B. JENNETT

Contributors

R. S. Downie, Professor of Moral Philosophy, Department of Philosophy, University of Glasgow, Scotland.

E. M. Eppel, Professor of Continuing Education and Director of the Centre for Continuing Education, Sussex University, England.

R. Gillon, Director, Imperial College Health Service, London University; Editor, *Journal of Medical Ethics*; Deputy Director, Institute of Medical Ethics; Senior Fellow, Centre for Medical Law and Ethics, King's College, London University, England.

H. ten Have, Professor of Philosophy, Department of Philosophy and Ethics of Health Care, Rijksuniversiteit Limburg, The Netherlands.

P. Hucklenbroich, Lecturer in Philosophy, Institut für Theorie und Geschichte der Medizin, Universität Münster, FRG.

W. B. Jennett, Professor of Neurosurgery, University of Glasgow, Scotland and King's Fund Institute, London, England.

A. McGuire, Fellow of the Socio-Legal Studies Centre and Pembroke College Oxford; formerly Research Fellow in Health Economics, Health Economics Research Unit, University of Aberdeen, Scotland.

G. Mooney, Professor of Health Economics, University of Aberdeen, Scotland and University of Copenhagen, Denmark.

H. D. C. Roscam Abbing, Part-time Professor in Health Law, Rijksuniversiteit Limburg, The Netherlands.

F. F. H. Rutten, Professor of Health Economics, Rijksuniversiteit Limburg, The Netherlands.

P. Sohl, Institute of Social Medicine, University of Copenhagen, Denmark.

J. Vang, Regional Officer for Health Technology Assessment, World Health Organization, Regional Office for Europe, Copenhagen, Denmark.

1

Introduction

FRANS RUTTEN

Economists believe that medical ethics is very much concerned with the individualistic considerations of virtue and duty and that it tends to emphasize the need for the individual doctor to do his utmost for the individual patient. The objective of economics is utilitarian and economists strive to maximize benefits to society given the resources available. It is clear that by pursuing the interest of an individual patient to the extreme, one would come into conflict with the objective of maximizing social benefits. This at least alleged controversy between medical ethics and economics formed the motive for my colleagues ten Have, McGuire, Mooney and myself to bring together philosophers, physicians, economists, epidemiologists, psychologists, sociologists, and experts in law and medical ethics, and organize an international workshop on various aspects of the relationship between medical ethics and economics. This volume contains a selection of papers, the original versions of which were presented at the workshop and which certainly benefited from the lively and thorough discussions which took place at the workshop.

As an introduction to this volume it may be useful to make a number of observations on the role of doctors in the health care systems of the present day, and on the extent to which they are influenced by medical ethical norms and guidelines. To set the scene I would like to use Mooney and McGuire's image of the doctor–patient relationship (Chapter 2). The doctor provides the patient with two items of service. First he gives him information about how various treatment modes might contribute to the patient's health status. In a discussion between doctor and patient, in which the latter might bring in his own assessment of costs and benefits associated with particular treatment modes, the treatment strategy is decided upon. The second item of service from doctor to patient is then the treatment of the patient by the doctor, or, what is becoming more and more common, one or more referrals to other colleagues for treatment. The important questions to be raised here are who decides about treatment and what motives are present. The agency concept, as developed within economics, proposes that the doctor is the main decision maker with respect to the choice of treatment strategy, and that his motives are influenced by the fact that he acts for at least two principals, namely the patient and society, or at least, in the latter case, a third-party payer.

1

At the micro-level the conflict between medical ethics and economics relates to the difficulty of the physician's serving both the interests of his patient and those of society. Although there is reason for concern about these conflicting roles for the doctor, I would say it is not really very productive to focus on this contrast. Ten Have (Chapter 3) very elegantly argues that medical ethics certainly cannot be considered as a simple set of rules and guidelines stressing the individual patient's perspective and Gillon (Chapter 9) very convincingly shows that there really does not exist a typical doctor who is only concerned with the welfare of the patients currently in his care without consideration of other and perhaps future patients.

It seems more profitable to consider how doctors can be persuaded to deliver not only effective but also efficient health care. In this respect Vang (Chapter 10) stresses the importance of incorporating certain elements of economics and statistics into the education of doctors which may help them in their difficult task. Hucklenbroich (Chapter 8) assesses the usefulness of medical expert systems to help doctors to improve their decision making. Of at least equal importance, I would say, are the systems of financial incentives under which doctors operate. In raising this I am thinking not only of the old discussion about how doctors' payment systems influence their behaviour. I would also like to stress the necessity to analyse the impact of a number of new developments in financial incentives on doctors' behaviour. One of these is the increasing importance of competitive arrangements in health care, as we see developing in the United States. Surely the fact that doctors have a stake in the economic performance of Health Maintenance Organisations, for-profit hospitals, preferred provider organizations, etc. does influence their behaviour. It has been observed, for instance, that doctors in these circumstances tend to use advanced technology more often, since one of the instruments for competitors in the market for health care is the degree to which they provide ready access to advanced medical technologies for their patients. Another important new phenomenon is the fact that doctors are increasingly facing legal claims from their patients involving considerable sums of money. This leads to so-called defensive medicine which is certainly not efficient medicine.

Having observed that doctors' behaviour is influenced by several factors, some of which may be used to promote their efficient behaviour, the question still remains of whether the doctor–patient relationship is special and whether the patient needs special protection as is intended to be provided by medical ethics. Downie (Chapter 4) takes a bold stand in this respect in arguing that such special protection is not needed and that on the contrary past experience with the use of medical ethical guidelines shows that these are often counter-productive. I would argue that his position becomes more and more defensible as health care technology proceeds and the autonomy of the patient is more and more stressed.

Medical technological development makes the doctor become increasingly someone who helps the patient in 'shopping around' in the health care system rather than simply being his personal physician. Some argue that the patient's permission to give his doctor access to his body makes his relation with the doctor quite special and leaves the patient in a vulnerable position and therefore in need of protection. This is less and less the case when medicine becomes more technical and access to the body is no longer given exclusively to one's own personal physician.

The second reason why medical ethics becomes less needed to protect the patient is the expected change in the doctor–patient relationship when the patient becomes better educated and more autonomous. Mooney and McGuire (Chapter 2) argue that the transfer of decision-making authority from patient to doctor may induce a utility of its own (process utility). The patient might not want to be faced with difficult decisions bearing large consequences for his health status. As information on health care provision to lay people increases, perhaps also in combination with increased competition, the doctor–patient relationship becomes similar to that of the butcher and the consumer (for some odd reason this analogy is often used!) or any other relationship in a 'normal' market. In that case the need for special protection in the form of medical ethical rules and guidelines becomes less pressing.

One should not infer from the previous observations that medical ethics does not have a role in modern medicine at all. On the contrary, medical ethics as a continuous effort to reflect on norms and values in health care seems essential, especially nowadays! On the one hand medical technological development has never before provided us with such a wide range of options for diagnostics and treatment, while on the other hand limits to the growth of health care expenditures have been approached. Together with utilitarian-based economics, medical ethics should provide guidance on how to use other ethical principles in answering difficult questions with respect to the use of new technologies and with respect to patient selection.

Turning away from the level of the doctor–patient relationship and considering the same issues at a higher level of decision making, one can observe an interesting discussion on the role of doctors in health care policy making. Mooney and McGuire suggest that, at all levels of decision making beyond that of the management of an individual doctor's patients, judgements about policy have to be made by society or its representatives rather than by medical doctors, who are not qualified or competent to act as society's representatives in defining these judgements. In practice doctors do influence decisions of policy makers to a large extent, depending on a particular system of policy making, and often their role as advisors to policy makers or even as decision makers themselves is firmly incorporated in decision-making structures.

Currently one may observe that the tension between medical technological options on the one hand, and limits to the resources available on the other, has triggered a discussion on how to deal with new, advanced medical technologies at the macro-level of decision making. One of the outcomes of this discussion is that technology assessment studies by multi-disciplinary teams of doctors, economists, and ethicists should be performed in the early stages of the diffusion of new technologies and that the consequent results should be taken into account when deciding about regulatory actions concerning the diffusion of these technologies. A second topic in the debate is the question of who will be the most prominent advisors in decision making about medical technology, and whether it is justifiable that doctors have a special position here.

As an example it is interesting to consider the discussion about the current position of the Health Council in the Netherlands. This council is the main advisor to the government about matters of health technology in a broad sense. On specific topics expert committees are formed within this council; these report on the state of the art with respect to a medical technology and its desired use. In recent years people from disciplines like economics, ethics, and law have been added to these committees, which used to be dominated by medical experts. As a consequence the Health Council's Reports have become broader and include socio-economic considerations, based on not only medical but also economic and other expertise. This development shows a way in which a reconciliation between medicine, medical ethics, and economics becomes possible and may prove to be beneficial for the quality of decision making in health care.

To my knowledge the International Workshop on Medical Ethics and Economics in Health Care has been the first attempt to bring together people from different disciplines to discuss systematically a number of different aspects of possible conflicts between the two disciplines. From this it follows that the authors in this volume had to enter into new territories and could not just follow already well-established lines of thought. This has added tremendously to the originality of the contributions in this volume, which the editors hope will help further to explore this interesting no man's land between ethics and economics.

2

Economics and medical ethics in health care: an economic viewpoint

GAVIN MOONEY and ALISTAIR MCGUIRE

Summary

This chapter attempts to analyse the relationship between medical ethics and economics. In particular the importance of medical ethics to the process of resource allocation in health care is studied. It is argued that medical ethics is often narrowly conceived in that the individual, rather than society at large, forms the focal point when medical ethics dominates the resource allocation process. This raises a conflict between the individualistic formulation of medical ethics and the objective of maximizing social benefits (i.e. the benefits in aggregate to all individuals in society), which is the goal of economic efficiency. It is suggested that the structure of the health care sector augments the individualistic aspects of medical ethics and helps to determine its importance in allocating resources in the health care sector. The conflict between social and individualistic ethical codes is discussed by considering the relationship between utilitarianism and medical ethics, placing particular emphasis upon the definition of process as an end-state to be taken into account in defining the maximization of social benefit.

Adopting this stance means that, in measuring the benefits of health care, we would advocate focusing on the social benefits which are to be measured, not solely in terms of health status improvements (i.e. outcome utility) but also in the reduction in risk bearing by patients in medical decision making (i.e. process utility). Medical ethics as currently practised too frequently emphasizes the individual qua *individual at the expense of individuals as society and ignores non-health status influences on utility. It is also all too pervasive in health care decision making and ought to be restricted to clinical decisions.*

2.1. Introduction

The aim of this chapter is to present a general outline of the interaction between the use of economics and the presence and practice of medical ethics in the health care sector. In doing so the chapter attempts to show that medical ethics has been dominated by 'individualistic' ethical codes which are not capable of considering questions relating to resource allocation at a social level. Consideration of these wider social questions involves issues of public choice. We present an analysis which shows that in the health care sector the present formulation of medical ethics acts as a constraint on this process. In doing this we first consider the importance of the ethical philosophy of utilitarianism and the role it plays in the resource allocation process. We then outline the structure of the health care sector, highlighting the importance of the clinician.

From this analysis the importance of medical ethics in health care resource allocation is highlighted. The conflict between the formulation of medical ethics as it focuses on the individual *qua* individual and the objective of maximizing social benefits (i.e. the benefits to that group of individuals called society) is then outlined.

2.2 Some economic concepts

The philosophical basis of most economics is utilitarianism. This is manifested in the fundamental tenet of economics that resource allocation should be aimed at maximizing the benefits to society from the resources available. In other words resources should be used in the most efficient manner possible. Recognizing that resources are limited and society's wants apparently insatiable results in the need to resolve which of the competing claims to the use of these resources should be accepted and which rejected. This consideration gives rise to the notion of opportunity cost, which states that there is always a cost or sacrifice when resources are used since there are always alternative, socially desirable uses to which the resources might otherwise have been put. In other words, the use of resources gives rise to a potential loss of benefit because opportunities are forgone. Efficiency consists of always attempting to maximize benefits or, conversely, minimize the benefits forgone whatever the resource limitations.

The end sought by economic policy—the maximization of benefits—is based upon an aggregation of the benefits, or to be precise the utility derived from the benefits gained by individuals from the resource allocation process. This emphasis on gains to individuals is important because it introduces the concept of consumer sovereignty into the resource allocation process. This concept assumes that it is the consumer of resources alone who is the best judge of the utility gained from the use of resources. Thus as well as being consequentialist (i.e. being concerned with the consequences or outcomes of different actions) economics also assumes that social welfare is an aggregation of individuals' utilities. This does not necessarily mean that utility can only be derived selfishly; it is quite possible to have interdependence across different individuals' utility functions.

Both benefit and the associated notion of cost will be recognized as value concepts. That is, in judging competing claims and the consequent (opportunity) costs and resultant benefits, we are dealing with the notion of value. In order to define this notion, we would distinguish between *value in use* and *value in exchange*, a distinction central to the subsequent arguments of the paper. Economics, or as it was formerly called, political economy, as defined by Mill for example, is concerned with value in exchange. Indeed it is worth quoting Mill at length:

Political economy has nothing to do with the comparative estimation of different uses in the judgement of a philosopher or a moralist. The use of a thing, in political economy, means its capacity to satisfy a desire or serve a purpose . . . The exchange value of a thing may fall short, to any amount of its value in use; but that it can ever exceed the value in use implies a contradiction; it supposes that persons will give, to possess a thing, more than the utmost value which they themselves put upon it as a means of gratifying their inclinations (1909, p. 437).

The importance of this distinction between value in use and value in exchange can be examined when comparing health and health care. Much confusion regarding values in this context stems from there being insufficient recognition that consideration of the value of health and the value of health care involves two different concepts of value. The first is value in use and the second is value in exchange. The distinction is important because from this it can be seen that, in line with the concept of consumer sovereignty, it is only the consumer/patient who can attach a value (in use) to health status. Furthermore, in that it is only health care which has exchange value, because health *per se* can not be traded in markets, it is only in the context of health care that the concept of opportunity cost can be applied. This distinction and its consequences are fundamental to any discussion of the economics of the health care sector.

2.3. Economics of the health care sector

The structure of the health care sector is significantly different from other structures, with the position of the medical doctor (hereafter doctor) assuming particular importance. The majority of the sectors of the economy exhibit simple two-way transactions between buyers and sellers. These transactions are defined by price and output (quantity) levels and a fairly clear distinction between the supply function and the demand function, and hence between producers and consumers. It is conventional to assume that the individual consumer is the best person to judge his own welfare. The consumers' willingness to pay for commodities—the concept of demand—is based upon their perceptions of the expected utility to be gained from the consumption of any good or service. Consumers are assumed to be sufficiently well informed to be able to make rational judgements on how to maximize their utility, which in turn is assumed to be what determines consumer behaviour.

Further, the information flows set up on the demand side of the market can be used to assist producers to supply those goods and services which will provide both utility for consumers and revenue for producers. These information flows, transmitted by the market, are an essential ingredient in the achievement of economic efficiency.

The health care sector is different in that the natures of both health and health care are such that consumers are faced with major uncertainties because of their ignorance of health states, the availability of treatments, and their likely effectiveness. As a result they have to rely much more upon the supplier, normally the doctor, to assist them in determining their appropriate demands. Obviously, if left to the market, the monopoly potential of the supplier over information concerning both health status and the interaction of health care and health status may be realized. To avoid any such realization the set of exchange relationships which are normally characterized by the market are replaced by various non-market relationships.

Of particular importance is the (non-market) agency relationship which exists between the doctor (the producer) and the patient (the consumer). The commodity of health care, from the patient and potential patient's standpoint, is characterized by uncertainty due to lack of information and, in addition, unpredictability and possibly irrationality given diminished health status at the time of consumption. Consequently, the consumer looks to the doctor for what are two separate but not independent commodities: information and treatment. It may be noted at this stage that consumers do not readily want to consume health care *per se*: health care is a 'bad'. Rather they wish to improve their non-tradable health status and this can only be achieved indirectly, predominantly through the consumption of health care. Thus the rational consumer normally does not want to consume treatment. Nor do consumers have the necessary information about the relationship between treatment and health status. The doctor can identify the necessary level of production of health care (i.e. the supply of treatment) and simultaneously, in his or her capacity as agent, specify to the patient the desirable amount of consumption of health care to improve health status and thereby influence the demand for treatment—although even here there is often uncertainty surrounding the relationship between the treatment and the outcome. Moreover it is of fundamental importance to recognize that, even so, it is only the patient who can determine the utility derived from the value in use attached to improve health status.

This last point is important, not least because it can now be seen that the patient and doctor are respectively demanding and supplying different things. While patients demand health status improvements which are non-tradable but can be derived from health care, they accept the provision of health care information and treatment by doctors. Recognition of not only the ignorance of the patient but also the derived demand aspect of consumption leads the doctor to supply information simultaneously on the technical relationship between health care treatment and health status. However, it is still only the patient (consumer) who can attach value to the potential improvement in health status.

There is an added complication. The doctor's assessment of the treatment requirements is not perfect. He thus becomes a part bearer in the risk of adverse outcome associated with the production process (i.e. the supply of treatments). Harris (1977, p. 473), in discussing the hospital from an economic perspective, describes this as a special negative externality whereby the doctor bears the 'moral burden of ultimate responsibilities for the outcome of the case'. This he suggests inevitably occurs 'in an arrangement in which one makes repeated marginal decisions about life and death'. There is a demand from the patient to shift risk bearing regarding outcome to the doctor and as part of the agency relationship an acceptance of this 'cost' by the doctor. Whether this demand is constant across different specialties or across hospital and primary care will not be debated in this paper.

The existence of the agency relationship and this risk-bearing function means that the doctor becomes a property rights holder in the patient's utility function. This notion of property rights holdings is fundamental to our analysis. Essentially such a holding is seen to arise from an entitlement to resource use, which is determined through the pertaining economic and social relations which define any individual's position with respect to the utilization of scarce resources. Property rights may be understood as the sanctioned behavioural relations among men that arise from the existence of goods and pertain to their use (Furubotn and Pejovich 1972). The doctor's property rights holdings in the patient's utility function allows him (the doctor) to help determine the level of consumption and thus the level of expected benefit, and consequently the utility to be attached to the commodity health care. However, these property rights remain indirect in that it is only the patient/consumer who can properly determine the relationship between health status and utility.

Thus in the consumption of health care the autonomy of the individual is threatened by the position occupied by the doctor. The patient has to trust that his doctor will act in his (the patient's) best interest. As part of a response to this market failure to cope with the characteristics of the commodity health care, the supply side of the market has been regulated in a manner which attempts to separate the doctor's medical behaviour from the resource implications of that behaviour. (The nature and extent of this separation cannot be viewed in isolation from the nature of the medical remuneration system, e.g. salary, fee-for-service, or per capitation fee.) Along with a tendency to pool the risks associated with the uncertainty concerning the loss of health status levels, this attempt to insulate medical decision making from economics has resulted, *inter alia*, in promoting financing by third parties.

Thus the conventional market, where the three functions of the individual consumer's 'cost–benefit calculus'—benefit receiving, cost bearing, and decision making—are performed by the individual, may be contrasted with the health care sector. Here the decision making may be delegated to the doctor, much of the cost-bearing function at the point of consumption may rest with the financing third party, and even the benefit-receiving aspect will in part be influenced by information from the doctor regarding the nature and size of the benefit.

The role of the doctor is then crucial because he is performing simultaneously on both sides of the market. While acting as an agent for the patient in the process of the demand for treatment, at the same time he specifies the supply of treatment. In doing so the doctor is constrained, by his acceptance of medical ethics, as discussed in detail in the next section, to determine the treatment through his role as agent and not, as would be the case for suppliers in other sectors of the economy, for self-gain, pecuniary or otherwise. While it is normal to assume that this is true across all financing and remuneration systems, the extent to which it is true may well vary with the system. Unlike other sectors there is little and indeed in most health care systems no analysis of the costs of production by the person specifying the level of production (treatments), that is, by the doctor.

To the extent that the doctor is concerned with opportunity costs, these will relate primarily to the individual treatment being specified at any particular point in time. In other words the view of opportunity cost to the medical profession, if considered at all, will be constrained, *ceteris paribus*, to the short run and to a narrow frame of reference (see Williams 1985). The institutional framework within which the doctor operates supports these constraints, although how it operates in practice may vary, depending for example, on whether the immediate concern is with, say, general practitioner or hospital clinician behaviour.

Hence given third-party payment when acting as an agent on the individual level, the doctor may not perceive the full opportunity cost and there will be a consequent loss in efficiency. Furthermore, in devoting some finite resources to an individual patient, the doctor is also undertaking a distributional function. Maximization of the benefits from health care requires that the doctor act as an agent for society, as well as an agent for the individual patient involved in the particular short-run production process (treatment), although the latter will dominate his concern at any specific point in time.

Thus it would seem that the individualistic behaviour of the doctor, which gains some support from the structure of the health care sector, leads one away from the normal resource allocation objective, that is, the maximization of benefits to society from the available resources. However, not all structures are the same in all countries and it is pertinent to discuss the extent to which different structures—organizational, legal, financing, etc.—influence the individualistic behaviour of individual doctors. This would seem to be an important yet underinvestigated area. However, in general such structures seem merely to support this 'individualistic' behaviour: they are not the foundation for it. To examine the foundations it is necessary to turn to consider medical ethics for, as we began to suggest above, it is here that the constraints on behaviour are dictated.

2.4. Medical ethics in health care provision

The last section outlined the importance of the structural environment in the determination of behaviour. In particular the agency relationship was seen to be central to an understanding of this behaviour. Indeed it is because of the existence of this relationship between the patient and the doctor that medical ethics assumes such importance, in as much as it delineates the normative boundaries of acceptable behaviour. (The extent to which differences in organizational, legal, and financing structures influence this relationship is likely to be important. Yet little seems currently to be known of such influences.) As such, Jonsen and Hellegers (1974) state that present medical ethics is individualistic in character, resting upon the concepts of virtue and duty. The poorly informed consumer, as discussed above, enters into an agency relationship in an effort to ascertain the required health care to improve health status. His lack of information means, however, that the consumer cannot evaluate performance on an *ex ante* basis. Medical ethics then provides reassurance that the doctor will attempt to do his best for the individual patient.

As Arrow has indicated 'the usual reasons why the market acts as a check to ensure quality operate here with very weak force. It is for this reason that ethical indoctrination of doctors is of such crucial importance. The control exercised ordinarily by informed buyers is replaced by internalised values' (Arrow 1963, p. 37). The legitimation of the doctor's property rights in the individual patient's utility function is thus gained directly through the medical ethical code. This legitimation is enhanced by the attempt within medical ethics to divorce the medical doctor from considerations of resource allocation, in other words to be concerned with the effectiveness of individual patient care rather than the social implications associated with the use of resources. The prime focus is the individual patient rather than the efficiency or the equity of aggregate care which is subject to resource constraints. The organization of hospital services as Harris (1977) describes it, 'is set up to protect the doctor from behaving as economic man', a description which appears to be largely true of all health care systems. These aspects can be seen to accord with the characteristic of virtue in medical ethics.

Medical ethics also plays a role at a more aggregate level in as much as it allows individual doctors to know that they have acted broadly as their peers would have done. This role of medical ethics arises directly from the transfer, alluded to earlier, of risk holdings from patient to doctor. Strictly this does nothing to reduce the risk holding of the individual doctor; it merely affects his perception of the cost of that risk holding. In other words the non-transferability of the risk bearing by doctors to other actors in the production process can mean that medical ethics is a part substitute for risk sharing. There is no opportunity in the health care sector for short-term specialization in risk bearing across different actors with different degrees of risk aversion.

In the longer run such specialization is possible particularly with respect to choice of specialty. We would hazard that risk bearing is greater in, say, surgery than in geriatrics. Consequently, *ceteris paribus*, it would be expected that more risk averse doctors would enter geriatrics and psychiatry than surgery and acute medicine. Having said this, we know of no study which has investigated this issue.

Medical ethics, when viewed from the perspective of the profession as a whole, may therefore be seen as a mechanism for self-regulation. This has an important bearing on the structure of the health care sector since the medical profession is in a position to influence both short-run and long-run allocative efficiency, particularly the former. It is thus important that the potential ability of doctors to exercise their monopoly position (regarding the supply of both information and treatments) is held in check. In this sense also medical ethics regulates medical conduct. Yet again it does nothing to reduce the risk holding of doctors. However, it may serve to reduce the variance of outcome and in this way act as an *ex ante* check on performance. Whether it does so equally across different financing systems or indeed across hospital and primary care sectors is not so clear.

These latter influences of medical ethics are operative at an aggregate level, but are derived from the individualistic agency relationship. That is, they conform to the aspect of duty. Thus whilst in essence they do function at an aggregate level they do not directly broach questions of social efficiency or equity. The fact that an ethic of the common good (i.e. the good of individuals as a society) is missing from, or at least deficient in, medical ethics is a source of concern for the attainment of these social goals. Jonsen and Hellegers (1974) argue that this lack results in an absence of 'the ethical issues arising from the intersection of multiple actions in institutions and society' (p. 12). They suggest that the reason the doctrine of the common good is needed is 'to consider . . . how the institutional structure can be designed so as to avoid conflict, how to reconcile discord, and how to compensate unjust harm'. As (utilitarian) economists we would also want such a doctrine to embrace efficiency. In an attempt to analyse the relationship between the ethic of the common good and the individualistic nature of medical ethics, the next section considers the relationship between utilitarianism and medical ethics.

2.5. Utilitarianism and medical ethics

Utilitarianism is frequently viewed as being built on two pillars: (i) individual consumer sovereignty, and (ii) the emphasis on utility being derived from what the individual receives ('outcome utility'). This section discusses both these and suggests that utilitarianism can and should be accommodated within health care and that to do so requires a change in either the nature or the legitimate territory of medical ethics.

On consumer sovereignty, Harsanyi suggests (1982, p. 55) that it is necessary 'to distinguish between a person's manifest preferences and his true preferences . . . the latter being those . . . he would have if he had all the relevant factual information, always reasoned with the greatest possible care and were in a state of mind conducive to rational choice'. The dangers of not adopting this stance have been pointed out by Sen and Williams (1982, p. 10): 'If people do not, in fact, get round to actually wanting what it would be rational for them to want, people may always be actually unsatisfied by the results of the correct policy'.

While simple in principle, this notion of what is in essence the justification for medical ethics has some problems in practice. In attempting to evaluate choices at a clinical level there are five variables which have to be considered in the pursuit of efficiency:

1. The changes in the states of the world in which we have an interest (i.e. changes in health status).
2. The probabilities associated with these states of the world.
3. Attitudes to risk and risk bearing.
4. The utilities associated with these states of the world.
5. Consequent changes in resource use.

Given our earlier discussion of the special nature of the commodity health care, the agency relationship, etc., the main focus of medical ethics at an informational level is to give the medical doctor certain property rights regarding health outcomes in the patient's utility function. Consequently as potential consumers of information regarding their own health status—essentially effectiveness—individuals seek the perfect agency relationship to allow them to obtain the appropriate information to allow decisions to be made more in line with their 'true preferences'.

The key issue here has been spelt out by Weisbrod (1978, p. 52) as follows:

What a buyer wants to know is the difference between his state of well-being with and without the commodity being considered. For ordinary goods, the buyer has little difficulty in evaluating the counter-factual—that is, what the situation will be if the good is not obtained. Not so for the bulk of health care (and legal representation, to cite another example) . . . The noteworthy point is not simply that it is difficult for the consumer to judge quality before the purchase (as it also is in the used car case), but that it is difficult even after the purchase.

With regard to attitudes to risk and risk bearing, this is a partially neglected aspect of the agency relationship. Yet, as the quote from Harris above indicates, it is a potentially important one. A large part of the reason why medical ethics, together with the agency relationship, is legitimized in the eyes of the patient is that it allows the patient to avoid bearing the risk associated with a decision-making process which may yield adverse outcomes. The anxiety involved in 'getting it wrong' and the associated moral responsibility are features which are crucial to acceptance of medical ethics. Additionally consumers may believe that, left to exercise their own preferences on risk, they might in practice be too risk averse for, literally, their own good.

Where individual autonomy remains and should remain is with respect to utility—although it may be necessary for the doctor to assist the patient in clarifying his (the patient's) assessment. The consideration of the importance of autonomy and its relationship to utility may be broached with regard to two important issues in the provision of health care.

First, where in most health care systems the medical doctor is most clearly not in a position to exercise his judgement at an individual level is with regard to costs, both those falling on the patient and those on the financing third party and society more generally. On the former the problems are obvious; on the latter both medical practice and medical ethics seek to protect the doctor from taking account of such resource considerations at any level.

Medical ethics consequently seems most readily applicable at the level of care of the individual patient and issues of effectiveness which are untrammelled by thoughts of non-medical constraints. Certainly it is difficult, and indeed contrary to the spirit of medical ethics at this individual level, to have medical ethics also playing a prominent role in issues of the efficiency of health care resources generally. But, given that there has to be *some* trade-off in terms of resource use across any individual doctor's patients, there are signs that medical ethics, as currently conceived, results in some problems even at that level.

Clearly, since they are not independent, there is a need to link effectiveness, the main focus of medical ethics, with efficiency, on which economics concentrates. In doing so, there is no uniquely correct way of achieving this. We would submit, however, that utilitarianism ought to be the basis of the decision-making process in health care, but a form of utilitarianism which differs in an important way from how it is perhaps conventionally viewed. What we mean by this will become clearer in considering autonomy, utility, and medical ethics in a second and different light.

Second, and as argued previously, the uncertainty surrounding the commodity health care results in important property rights being vested in medical doctors, in terms of their ability to enter the patient's utility function. At the same time we have stressed that such an ability is largely restricted to the direction of the patient's determination of the utility associated with changes in his health status. What justifies the importance of the doctor's property rights in this context is the fact that the patient is prepared to give up his property rights regarding the risk bearing arising from the uncertainty associated with outcome. It is this property right holding in another individual's utility function which leads to a necessary amendment of the basic utilitarian stance.

Utilitarianism is often viewed as being based on utility derived *solely* from what is obtained (i.e. 'outcome' utility). It is because of this that it is frequently attacked on grounds that the end is used to justify the means. This restriction to outcome utility is disputed by some utilitarians, particularly on the issue of the utility derived from freedom of choice. For example, Hahn suggests (1982, p. 188) 'my utility may not only depend on what I (and others) get but on the manner in which I get it. That is why utility may not only depend on the consequences of policy but on the policy itself'. The example he used is as follows (*op. cit.* p. 189):

Suppose that I give a certain amount to a particular charity. The government decides to tax me to that amount and gives it to the same charity. Am I indifferent between these two situations? Before the tax, I had the possibility of acting otherwise than I did even though I chose not to, after tax the possibility is gone. But even if one attaches no probability to wishing to avail oneself of a possibility, its loss by restricting one's potential freedom may be felt as a loss of utility.

This is a classic case of the utility of freedom of choice or individual autonomy. Indeed some take the view that even if the individual were to do himself harm and after the event *know* that he had done himself harm because he had acted on the basis of poor information, none the less he would have suffered disutility if someone had interfered with his freedom of choice. Consumer autonomy enters the individual's utility function, in addition to the utility of the choice of the outcome. For example, Mishan (1971) states:

Person A may find himself disabled for life and rue his decision to take the risk. But this example is only a painful reminder of the fact that people come to regret a great many of the choices they make, notwithstanding which they would resent any interference with their future choices.

There is neither in principle nor in practice an insuperable problem here. If people do derive utility (positive *or* negative) from the process through which they receive a particular outcome then such process utility is relevant in deciding on how that person's overall utility is both measured and maximized. If this is the case (and it seems to us intuitively likely) it is clearly not enough to consider only *outcome* utility; *process* utility must be considered as well.

A crude example demonstrates one aspect of this. On average, let us say that each day one defenceless child is killed on the roads. In driving on any particular day each driver knows there is some probability, small but positive, that he can kill a defenceless child. Yet people drive. Were an individual to know *with certainty* that in driving he would be the one to kill a defenceless child and he still chose to drive, the situation would have changed markedly—even although *ex post* the outcome is the same, namely that one child is dead. Whatever the specific reason for this change, we believe the important point is that it can be encapsulated in process utility. By this term is meant what we think utilitarians frequently mean by it, that is, it is not just the utility of the output that matters: the utility of the process that results in the output is also relevant.

With regard to health care consumption there is a disutility for the patient if he has to bear the risk associated with decision making about his health care. For the individual consumer there are perceived high costs of decision making in the form of anxiety about the probability of getting it wrong, the state of the world if he does get it wrong, and the burden of responsibility of getting it wrong. In the context of process utility the wish to shift this burden of responsibility may well be strong. The fact that this responsibility can be avoided by passing the risk-bearing function to the medical doctor means that the individual is prepared to trade this gain in utility against the loss associated with a dimunition of his autonomy. These aspects of utility and disutility are different in kind from those associated with the outcome (the change in health status). In this sense, the indirect involvement in the patient's utility function by the doctor results in this process itself becoming a source of utility, as well as a means towards improved health status. This process utility is particularly important given that health care is a 'regrettable'.

A second form of process utility may also be important. Generally it is possible to incorporate equality in the utilitarian position by assuming each individual's utility has equal importance, that is, that social welfare is simply the sum of individuals' utilities. However, in health care, beyond this instrumentalist view, equality may additionally be considered as a 'morally desirable feature' (a phrase borrowed from Scanlon (1977, p. 143) who discusses similar issues in a wider context). Equality is thus viewed as another form of process utility associated with the delivery of health care and as such is seen as a separate identity in the utility function.

Against this background of the notion of process utility as related to equality, the doctor's dominance in the decision-making process, on both consumption and production levels, becomes important in this context, as well as in the risk-bearing context discussed above. Society needs someone to operationalize its policy on equity. Doctors appear well placed to assume this role and society appears prepared to invest the property rights regarding the implementation of equity goals in the doctor in his 'gatekeeper' capacity. The doctor is then acting on a distributional and not just purely medical level, but for the individual as a citizen rather than as a consumer. Yet, interestingly, it is the agency role of the doctor *vis-à-vis* the *consumer* arising from the information asymmetry and the simultaneity of production and consumption decisions which places the doctor in the position to be able to play the role of society's agent on implementing (but not in any way shaping) policy on equity.

Accepting this position means recognizing that potential trade-offs exist between equity and efficiency. The pursuit of any particular notion of equity adopted, or the way in which the concept of equity is implemented, may interfere with the efficiency with which any outcome is achieved.

It must be stressed, however, that the potential trade-offs between equity and efficiency can only be resolved at the social level. Whilst the doctor may indeed 'realize' this trade-off, that is, be crucial in the implementation of the process, the rights to enact this implementation are assigned by society. At times when resource constraints are not binding such trade-offs may be made smoothly and the fundamental property rights holdings not called into question. However, when resource constraints tighten then disputes over property rights holdings and the control over trade-offs are bound to occur. The property rights to the realization of the process utility associated with equality (say of access) do indeed give the doctor a strong position in the resource allocation decision-making process. However, if society, for example in the form of government, starts to adjust the trade-off between equity and efficiency, it may be that the clinician, who retains a predominant interest in his immediate customer (patient), may be unwilling to release his property rights holdings, even though these have only been assigned by society and even though his realization of this assignment is now at odds with social objectives.

The discussion of process utility raises considerable implications for the concept of autonomy, particularly in that many have defended the concept of greater autonomy for consumers in health care. But the question of autonomy over *what*, needs more careful examination than it has hitherto received. Whether to opt for increased autonomy hinges not solely on the utility associated with that freedom but also on the overall utility including both outcome and process utility. Given the difficulties that individuals have in making choices about health care consumption, autonomy may well have a negative utility in some instances. At the most basic level, for example, autonomy will involve search costs, the avoidance of which might be more highly valued than the resultant benefits. However, it is more the psychological costs of exercising such autonomy (in other words the fear of getting it wrong) that may be important in this context. Note that whilst the consumer suffers a loss in autonomy, because only he can attach value (in use) to health status, there is no loss in consumer sovereignty.

The ethical stance adopted by the medical doctor, based as it is upon the aspects of virtue and duty, the process utility to the patient, and the dominant position of the doctor in the health care sector, are complementary. Indeed the structure of the sector supports these complementary positions, in that it is dominated by the individualistic benefit-maximizing forces. Thus even at an aggregate level the medical profession have looked upon self-regulation in terms of potential abuse of monopoly power at the individual level, rather than being concerned with any wider social aspects of efficiency or equity. The goal of maximization of benefits requires the medical practitioner to act as an agent of society as well as of the patient. However, this role may undermine the property rights holding in the individual patient's utility function and in this sense is in potential conflict with the other aspects encompassed by medical ethics, that is, the separation of clinical interests from economic interests, the *ex ante* performance evaluation role, the risk bearing and associated involvement in the consumer's utility function. It is difficult to see how to widen the role of medical ethics to encompass an ethic of the social good without potentially endangering the 'ends' aspects of process utility in health care.

2.6. Conclusion

We have tried to highlight some of the tensions between medical ethics and economics in decision making in health care and in particular why they exist. The source appears to be the very nature of the commodity health care and the major uncertainties surrounding it as perceived by the patient.

It is both because of this uncertainty and in an effort to ameliorate the problems associated with it that medical ethics exists. Medical ethical codes, while highly desirable at this level, cease to be so if they are used to override wider considerations of social efficiency and social equity. It has to be clear that the aggregation of each individual doctor's clinical freedom in pursuit of the best health of his patients is unlikely to sum to the greatest benefit to society as a whole nor to anything that might be equated with just health care.

Indeed implicit in this view of individual good for patients is an assumption that there are no interdependencies of utility across different patients. This means that beyond the issue of helping to *implement* social policy on equity in both principle and practice, medical practice and medical ethics appear to have nothing to say about distributive justice in health care, which, as normally conceived, is based either on interdependent utilities as a result of a caring externality (individuals are concerned for others' health or access to health care) or a desire on the part of individuals to do their fair share for society at large (and hence contribute to allowing all to have access to health care)—that is, a form of process utility. Since distributive justice like efficiency is a matter of *social* concern the lack of relevance of medical ethics to it is understandable, but perhaps surprising.

When they become involved in policy making and enter debates about relative social values for the care of different groups of patients, medical doctors therefore appear to be going beyond their area of competence. They are not well placed to form judgements about social opportunity costs which inevitably involve social judgements, albeit ethical ones. These are judgements which need to be made by society or its representatives, and medical doctors are simply not qualified or competent to act as society's representatives in defining these judgements. Indeed currently and rightly medical ethical codes, in arguing for the individual doctor to do the best for his patients, endorse the lack of competence of doctors to perform in this way. Such codes do not always, as we illustrated earlier, support this logic.

In presenting these views, as one of us has written elsewhere (McGuire 1986):

If the ethic of the common good could be internalised within *prima facie* duty for the individual doctor, it would mean that the doctor *ought* to weigh up the social costs and benefits associated with each individual treatment, i.e. there would be reconciliation of individual and social utilitarian objectives. However the doctor is constantly faced with the short-run allocation problems. The individual ethical aspects of virtue and duty which underpin the non-market relationships centred upon the clinician (i.e. the agency relationship and the self-government aspect) lead to strong property rights holdings in the production *and* consumption processes in the health care sector. This probably means that there is little hope of such an internalisation of the ethic of the common good. This ethic still has a role to play, *but in its own right*, and predominantly as a legitimisation of the aspect of self-government for the profession. Therefore, not surprisingly, its role is normally subjugated to the ethics of virtue and duty.

Decision making on social matters should legitimately be vested in society's chosen representatives. We would submit that there needs to be a line drawn between medical ethics and social ethics in health care. That line is best drawn at all levels of decision making beyond that of individual patient management and the management of an individual doctor's patients.

Elements of efficiency are present at this latter level and we would want to have these strengthened and encouraged through appropriate budgetary arrangements and output measurement. Beyond that we would advocate a health care ethical code based on cost–benefit analysis to ensure that the property rights regarding social decision making in health care are more firmly separated from the property rights vested in medical doctors as a result of their medical ethics (Mooney 1986). Such a code is needed for very similar reasons to those suggested for a medical ethical code, except that the emphasis moves from the consumer's concern to the citizen's concern. As citizens, individuals face uncertainty regarding the supply of health care and its efficient and equitable operation. They need to be reassured that the health care system is operating in their best interests (their in this context meaning the community as a whole) and that they can rely on those responsible to divine what is their best interests.

The countervailing influence of the health care ethical code would result in little need for change in the nature or principles of medical ethics. It would simply restrict the role of medical ethics in determining resource allocation patterns in the health care sector. A health care ethical code would seek to augment the decision-making process in health care, essentially through the explicit introduction of efficiency considerations. The difficulty is to reconcile this utilitarian stance with the moral obligations as outlined by medical ethics. We have not dealt with the mechanisms through which the trade-offs between the behaviour implied by such a reconciliation would occur. It is sufficient to state that such mechanisms would have to be supported at the social and individual level.

Acknowledgements

We are grateful to various members of HERU and to Elizabeth Russell (Department of Community Medicine, Aberdeen) for comments on earlier papers on this topic. Our thanks to Isabel Tudhope for typing the paper. We also wish to acknowledge financial support from the Scottish Home and Health Department for HERU activities.

Bibliography

As well as literature referred to in the text we have listed some books and papers which we have found useful in formulating our ideas.

Aaron, H. J. and Schwartz, W. B. (1984). *The painful prescription: rationing hospital care*. Brookings Institute, Washington.

Arrow, K. J. (1963). Uncertainty and the welfare economics of medical care. *American Economic Review* **53**, 941–73.

Arrow, K. J. (1974). Government decision-making and the preciousness of life. In Tancredi, L. R. (ed.) *Ethics of medical care*. Institute of Medicine, Washington DC.

Beauchamp, T. L. and Childress, J. F. (1979). *Principles of biomedical ethics*. Oxford University Press, Oxford.

Evans, R. G. (1985). *Strained mercy: the economics of Canadian health care*. Butterworths, Toronto.

Furubotn, E. and Pejovich, S. (1972). Property rights and economic theory: a survey of recent literature. *Journal of Economic Literature* **10**, 1138–59.

Gillon, R. (1986). *Philosophical medical ethics*. John Wiley and Sons, Chichester.

Hahn, F. (1982). On some difficulties of the utilitarian economist. In Sen, A. and Williams, B. (eds) *Utilitarianism and beyond*. Cambridge University Press, Cambridge.

Hahn, F. and Hollis, M. (eds) (1979). *Philosophy and economic theory*. Oxford University Press, Oxford.

Harris, J. (1977). The internal organisation of hospitals: some economic implications. *Bell Journal of Economics* **8**, 467–82.

Harsanyi, J. C. (1982). Morality and the theory of rational behaviour. In Sen and Williams, *op.cit.*

Jonsen, A. R. and Hellegers, A. E. (1974). Conceptual foundations for an ethics of medical care. In Tancredi, L. R. *op.cit.*

Kennedy, I. (1983). *The unmasking of medicine*. Paladin Granada, London.

McGuire, A. (1986). Ethics and resource allocation: an economist's view. *Social Science and Medicine* **22**, 1167–74.

McGuire, A. and Mooney, G. (1985). Ethics and property rights in the NHS hospital. Health Economics Research Unit *Discussion Paper No. 02/85*, University of Aberdeen.

Mill, J. S. (1909). *Principles of political economy* (new edition). Longman, Green & Co., London.

Mishan, E. (1971). *Cost–benefit analysis*. Allen and Unwin, London.

Mooney, G. (1986). *Economics, medicine and health care*, Wheatsheaf, Brighton.

Robbins, L. (1932). An essay on the nature and significance of economic science. MacMillan, London.

Scanlon, T. M. (1977). Rights, goods and fairness. *Erkenntnis*, **II**, May, 81–94 (also reprinted in Waldron, J. (ed.) *Theories of rights* 1984, Oxford University Press, Oxford)

Sen, A. and Williams, B. (1982). *Utilitarianism and beyond*. Cambridge University Press, Cambridge.

Tancredi, L. (ed.) (1974). *Ethics of medical care*. Institute of Medicine, Washington DC.

Veatch, R. M. (1981). *A theory of medical ethics*. Basic Books, New York.

Waldron, J. (ed.) (1984) *Theories of rights*. Oxford University Press, Oxford.

Weisbrod, B. (1978). Comment on M. V. Pauly. In Greenberg, W. (ed.) *Competition in the health care sector*. Proceedings of a conference sponsored by Bureau of Economics, Federal Trade Commission, Germanstown, Aspen Systems.

Williams, A. (1985). Medical ethics, health service efficiency and clinical freedom. *Nuffield/York Portfolios, Folio 2*. Nuffield Provincial Hospital Trust, London.

3

Ethics and economics in health care: a medical philosopher's view

HENK TEN HAVE

Summary

In this chapter it is argued that the notion of medical ethics commonly used by health economists is one of ethics as a set of rules for physicians' conduct. However, it is important to make a distinction between ethics as a product (the deontology of the medical profession) and ethics as a process (a reflection on the norms and values of medicine). Recent developments in society and health care made medical ethics in the first sense problematical; they gave rise to a notion of health care ethics in the latter sense. It then became important to analyse and clarify the moral principles involved. The relevant principles which are determined by the differing professional perspectives of physicians and economists are discussed in the chapter. These perspectives imply a difference of levels on which health and disease, caring and curing are approached. Physicians are operating at the treatment level which is focused on the individual good. Because their overriding obligation is to the individual patient they cannot be expected to take economic aspects into account. The economic framework, within which physicians operate, must be determined by public discussion at the policy level.

3.1. Introduction

Medicine and economics have entered into relationships only recently, unwillingly and *a contre-coeur*. These relations are at the same time inevitable and problematical, from a medical as well as an economic point of view. Both disciplines are apparently forced into co-operation, or at least peaceful coexistence. Thus there is the need to examine the sources of their friction and to elucidate the backgrounds of the *prima facie* incompatibility.

Such at least is the opinion prevailing in recent health economics literature. A plausible theory attributes the enmity between economics and medicine to the different ethical bases on which the two disciplines are

23

founded. Indeed, medical ethical codes and declarations used to be averse
to any economic consideration. These codes stipulated the duties of
doctors, such as the duty to maintain the highest standards of professional
conduct or to practice their profession uninfluenced by motives of profit. In
the interest of the patient every physician ought to act according to these
codified duties, irrespective of social circumstances and economic restrictions. The physician's autonomy is taken as the precondition of responsible
professional care. This is clearly stated for instance in two of the twelve
principles of social security and medical care, adopted by the World
Medical Assembly in 1963: 'The moral, economic and professional *independence* of the doctor should be *guaranteed*; . . . In the higher interest of
the patient there should be *no* restriction of the doctor's right to prescribe
drugs or any other treatment deemed necessary'. It is just this autonomy
which is questioned more and more from an economic perspective. Taking
this point of view it is quite understandable that the difficulties arising from
the strained relations between medicine and economics are reduced to one
central problem: a conflict between social and individualistic ethical bases.

But is this a correct description of the problem? Does it make clear what
moral issues are involved, what fundamental values we have to balance
against one another, and how we can make choices between these morally
compelling alternatives? Does it assume one specific framework of principles and values as overriding, and on what grounds?

3.2. Medical ethics and product

Debating the role of medical ethics in a particular context is often complicated by the ambiguity of the term 'ethics'. Traditionally, 'medical ethics' is
used to refer to the *deontology* of the medical profession, to 'codes of
conduct which consist partly of ordinary moral rules, partly of rules of
etiquette, and partly of rules of professional conduct' (Downie 1974). In
this sense medical ethics has three characteristics.

1. It is related to the professionalization of medicine. It was not until the
   late Middle Ages that we could speak of the development of a clearly
   defined medical deontology. As professionalization increased, physicians sought official recognition, resisting the claims of competing
   groups of medical practitioners. In this process emphasis placed on the
   common good was combined with an appeal to the self-interest of the
   members of the profession. Restricting the practice of medicine to a
   relatively small group of well-educated men was justified as a service to
   the public interest; society was protected against incompetent care and
   unscrupulous, profit-motivated practitioners (Bullough 1966). It seems
   obvious that recognition could only be gained on the condition of a

strong internal organization and self-imposed standards of behaviour. Self-regulation and a special style of life, put in terms of high ideals, duties and virtues, could promote the professional image, and thus the income, power, and prestige of each member. It is considered the task of professional organizations to supervise the proper conduct of physicians, to compose up-to-date codes of ethics and to publish regularly revised ethics manuals. It is apparently from the sixteenth century, when medicine was recognized as a profession, that the use of the word 'ethical' to refer to organizational rules and regulations is derived.[1]

2. Since it was primarily concerned with formulating standards of professional behaviour, medical ethics has been segregated for a long time from general intellectual history (Fox 1979). For example, whereas John Locke contributed to the development of political economy, from the eighteenth century physicians did not participate in the elaboration of economic doctrines. The same is true of the relations between medical ethics and (moral) philosophy until recently: the practical concerns of medicine were not looked upon as interesting food for philosophical thought.

3. Before the 1960s, ethics was not a subject which was frequently discussed in the medical literature. The various codes had not been subjected to major revisions. Apparently, there was a consensus of opinion about the moral commitments in medical care. Codification of professional conduct seems possible only if basic principles are generally accepted; it makes explicit, at least partly, what moral values are shared by members of a particular profession.[2]

In their critical discussions about medical ethics, health economists usually refer to the term in this traditional sense. Williams (1985) blames 'the dictates of medical ethics' for thwarting the drive for greater efficiency in providing health care. In Mooney's (1983) explanation of the incompatibility of medical ethics and economics, the words 'medical ethics' and 'medical ethical codes' are interchangeable. Also in McGuire and Mooney (1985) 'medical ethics' is understood as an 'aspect of clinical conduct', and used as a synonym for 'ethical standards of the medical profession' and 'ethical code'.[3] In these publications the prevailing conception of medical ethics is that of a product: a clear-cut and acknowledged collection of prescriptions for professional conduct, a set of rules which could be written down, and in fact usually is, in a handbook or a code.

However, it is questionable whether working with such a conception is appropriate in view of the current state of affairs in philosophy of medicine. Nor does it seem adequate for the aims of these authors. It cannot be denied that serious moral conflicts arise from a confrontation between medicine and health economics, and that economic considerations are too easily treated by the medical profession as of little importance and relevance or even as dangerous. Health economists' criticisms are not so much invalid, as in my opinion misdirected. There is indeed a clash of moral convictions but not because of doctors' clinging to an antiquated and inefficient code of ethics, but by virtue of the peculiar characteristics of a medical (as distinct from an economic) perspective—a perspective which is determined by the very nature of medicine as well as the goals of a healing relationship.

Before trying to incorporate an economic point of view within an enlarged medical perspective or to restore the unstable two-legged stool of medical ethics with a third leg,[4] we must carefully study economics and medicine as two distinct perspectives on health and disease, care and cure, each with its specific moral principles and *prima facie* reasons.

3.3 Medical ethics and process

Let me first of all adduce some arguments against a conception of medical ethics as a product.

1. Since the 1960s medical ethics has gone through various phases, gradually turning away from traditional deontology (ten Have and van der Arend 1985). At the outset this development was induced by internal reasons: the technological and scientific advances of medicine began to call forth an uneasiness within the profession itself. The conventions of clinical practice seem inadequate because of the revolutionary progress of medical science, and physicians themselves are seen to call for a new ethical awareness. However, the traditional profession-orientated ethics remains a strong influence. The new moral problems (artificial life support, abortion, euthanasia, experimentation on human subjects) are classified in a medically inspired taxonomy. Yet even those medical authors who recognized the need for reflection on the applications and moral consequences of medical knowledge did not allow for philosophical and moral interference in the internal affairs of medicine. The attitude and virtue of the practising physician were considered as the best guarantee for reliable medical care. Yet there was increasing strain on the traditional standards of behaviour.

   The next phase came about for external reasons. The recent and unprecedented power of medicine generated problems not only for the individual patient and physician but for society as well. This is reflected in the agenda for medical ethics, with a new variety of topics (e.g. costs of health care and allocation of resources, the moral qualities of the health care delivery system, ethical issues associated with health education and prevention, principles for health policy). It is also illustrated by the fact that the number of publications on moral problems in medicine written by non-physicians increased. Consequently the scope of medical ethics is considerably enlarged; there are new and more complex moral issues and new participants in an intensified moral debate. Medical ethics can be subsumed in a new category, viz. health care ethics, dealing not only with the problems arising in the doctor–patient relationship, but also with the moral problems of other health care professionals, with the moral issues created by the system of health care, and with the public affairs implications of biomedical development.

By the end of the 1970s there was a third, gradual change in ethical discussions. The importance of general philosophical issues for medicine was recognized, and consequently the need for a philosophical basis for health care ethics. Analysis of moral dilemmas inevitably raised questions about the nature of health and disease, and the goals of medicine. The moral problems of contemporary biomedicine were in this phase linked with a philosophically inspired taxonomy of topics, including autonomy, personhood, justice, coercion. Ethical evaluation of the doctor's thoughts and actions would be more penetrating when attended by an analytical dissection of his/her presuppositions and by a critical examination of the conceptual foundations of clinical practice. Ethicists as well as physicians pointed out that the moral issues of modern health care are embedded in philosophies of medicine as a practical human activity.

To conclude, in the past decades we have witnessed the gradual emergence of a new conception of medical ethics, viz. that of an activity or process of systematic and continuous reflection on the norms and values guiding medical theory and praxis, as part of a more encompassing health care ethics.

2. It is doubtful whether there exists yet a medical ethics in the traditional sense of a uniform deontology, valid for all members of the medical profession, or at least all clinicians. And if it exists, we can be sceptical about its significance and impact. For instance, professional organizations' codes of ethics have been revised several times since their adoption, but at this moment it has become almost impossible to design an ethical code which is both acceptable to the majority of physicians and which deals adequately with the range of moral issues facing today's medical practitioners (Ballantine 1979). In fact the more recent a code, the less detailed it is, and the less ethical guidance it provides in professional conduct. And even if an ethical imperative has been explicitly included in a code, we may not assume that doctors do actually behave in accordance with that imperative.

So I have my doubts about the genuine existence of a medical ethics in the sense of a monolithic and generally accepted deontology. Formerly it was the identifiable product of an implicit consensus as to professional obligations and correct behaviour. Nowadays such a consensus is lost.

3. Even if it were possible to reach a consensus in matters of virtuous conduct, professional obligations, and responsibilities in medicine, we can wonder why it is desirable to codify the results and present them as the product of moral reasoning. Medical ethics in this sense is usually too idealistic. It posits philanthropic ideals which cannot be translated into obligations to concrete patients. It is considered as a binding ideal for the profession. But what is its normative force? Why should the choices and decisions related to professional behaviour be based primarily on a shared ethical code? If they are, what is the role of individual personal values? We are living in a society with a pluralistic value system. As a consequence, medical ethics (in the sense of product) can claim or prescribe certain decisions that cannot be taken by an individual physician. Moral conflicts cannot be solved by following the dictates of medical ethics, as long as the individual ethical conscience is highly esteemed, as is the case in the pluralistic system of many Western societies (van der Arend 1987).

Codification of professional conduct raises another problem, viz. that of the juridicalization of ethics. Ethical codes can be used (and actually are used) as a remedy at law, whilst medical ethics presents itself as a system of enforceable rules and directives. These tendencies disregard the distinction between law and ethics. What is not prohibited by law is not *ipso facto* ethically allowed. The conception of medical ethics as a product leads to the idea that everything that is morally required has been done if the rules and obligations specified in it have been followed.[5]

On the other hand, medical ethics may function as an argument to legitimize to society the authority and power of the medical profession. However, it can only do so if the provision of services is related to the basic values of liberal society. Norms for professional roles are justified by their promoting and preserving these values.[6] If professional norms apply only to a particular group, then what is ethically correct for professionals would be independent of what is correct for others. In that case it would be very difficult to justify professional norms. It is understandable that the public demands an accounting from the medical profession of its performance in delivering health care. References to medical ethics (as a product) or ethical codes will no longer be satisfactory as they are designed to favour only professionals. They can be used to put an end to any discussion about norms and values, or to evade moral reasoning. What is needed is ethics as a process, particularly one of weighing the value(s) the medical profession promotes against the values of patients and others in society.

3.4. The methodology of ethics

Once we have chosen a conception of medical ethics as a process, the question arises of how moral reasoning proceeds and what purpose it has in medical matters. While limitations of space prevent my outlining it here in detail, the method of medical ethics has at least three steps: clarification, analysis, and recommendation (Beauchamp and Childress 1983; Harron *et al.* 1983; Beauchamp and McCullough 1984).

First of all, pivotal concepts need clarification to determine exactly what the moral problem is. Then we spell out the variety of conflicting principles and moral rules that are involved in this situation; we also examine the arguments for deciding one way or the other. We break up the overall structure of the problem into its leading alternatives and assess the pros and cons of these alternatives by balancing them one against the other. In the third, prescriptive phase, we organize disparate practices and *ad hoc* principles into a coherent and structured moral system, providing clearer guidance to practice and behaviour. We recommend a certain resolution of the moral dispute or a decision on what to do in this situation, showing the arguments and good reasons on which this recommendation is grounded.

In these phases, moral reasoning involves pursuing rules, principles and theories in an orderly way. Trying to determine which course of action is right, we provide good and sufficient moral reasons to justify a particular action. Reasons appeal to moral rules, which state that actions of a certain kind ought (ought not) to be done because they are right (wrong), and to moral principles.[7] Rules are justified by principles, which in turn are justified by comprehensive ethical theories (utilitarian and deontological theories). Principles and rules are action guides. Medical ethics seeks to provide good reasons for action through the medium of moral principles, thereby transcending personal attitudes and individual beliefs.

Although moral reasoning introduces clarity and consistency, its method has a serious weakness. In today's society two or more moral principles may conflict, and irresolvable moral dilemmas result. Moral reasoning itself provides no criterion or algorithm for choosing between conflicting principles. Which principle has priority often appears to be determined by the religious, professional or political ideas of a particular individual. Moral reasoning can tell us what the general principles are but not how we must prioritize them. Moral principles generate a range of moral reasons for and against (courses of) actions but we possess no rational way of weighing the claims of one principle against another (MacIntyre 1981).

So what is the value of reasoning in ethics if moral reasons are not particularly compelling? This is a matter of intense discussion in the philosophical literature and I can only briefly touch upon it here.[8] If a moral point of view implies forsaking pure egoism and a willingness to consider other people's interests, then most people can not be indifferent to the considerations adduced by moral reasoning. Reasoning offers reasons to people, but people are not always reasonable. As Warnock (1971) concludes: 'a person is moral, by and large, exactly in proportion as he really wants to be so'.

3.5 Differing viewpoints

It follows from the discussion above that health economists who criticize medical ethics as a product do so by having recourse to medical ethics as a process (or, more precisely, health care ethics). They very properly observe how the moral principles which they recognize as basic are in conflict with the fundamental principles guiding the professional behaviour of doctors. They wonder which principles are overriding and in what kind of situation. Because of the plurality of principles they have to weigh moral reasons.

Basic moral principles are independent principles which cannot be subsumed in each other or anything else. The independence of these principles can be attributed to the differing goals people seek to achieve in the course of their life. Goals in life are individual; they are a function of what sort of person we are. But they are also related to our station in life, particularly the profession to which we feel committed. Both health economists and physicians are seeking to work towards amelioration of the human predicament but they differ as to the specific ends at which they aim. The ends they are pursuing are determined by their professional viewpoints.

In order to catalogue the moral conflicts which could possibly arise, we have first of all to direct our attention to the characteristics of these viewpoints. In advance it is obvious that the viewpoints are different because of the disparity in the levels on which health and disease, caring and curing are approached.

The perspective of medicine

The moral principles to which physicians appeal reflect at least two types of philosophical assumptions: about the nature of illness and about the nature of medicine.

Illness is taken as a sign of the vulnerability of the human (which is the *a priori* condition for the existence of medicine). An ill person perceives an altered state of existence and experiences a disruption of his organism in relation to the world. Illness is, in the words of Pellegrino (1979), 'an ontological assault': it disrupts the unity of body and self, because the body impedes our choices and actions; the body is interposed between us and reality. When we get ill, we perceive an inability to cope with everyday life. Consequently, illness implies a loss of some freedoms.[9] That is why the subject has a need for help. The fact of illness determines the need for a relationship with a physician. Medicine is founded on a unique relationship in which one person seeks the aid of another. For this reason, the nature of medicine has been understood since ancient times in a rather idealistic, almost exalted sense.

Medicine can be defined as 'a relation of mutual consent to effect individualised well-being by working in, with, and through the body' (Pellegrino and Thomasma 1981; Thomasma 1983a, 1984a). From the special nature of this interpersonal relationship arises the special obligation for the person giving the aid to consider the best interests of the person seeking the aid. However, there is a lot of philosophical discussion about the proper end of medicine. Pellegrino summarizes his position as follows: the end of medicine is 'a right and good healing action taken in the interests of a particular patient' (Pellegrino 1979). This view, which is presented in similar terms by many authors, allows, however, for different interpretations.[10] Medicine's goal is healing, not necessarily curing, but few agree on the definition of health. Health is not merely a biological condition, but a fundamental value, regarded as a means for other more highly regarded values, and considered a necessary even if not sufficient condition for our well-being. Health is subject to personal and social interpretation. This means that expert and patient conceptions of health can differ. Individuals can have varying views on the good life. It also means that medicine is an expression of culture. Our concern for and about health is part of our cultural heritage and determined by the basic values of Western liberal societies. The specific form that healing takes in each society is intimately related to the central beliefs and values in that particular culture. It is therefore important to recognize that medicine (and its moral principles) must work within a socio-cultural framework; the individual physician–patient interactions are included in a more encompassing set of societal institutions and cultural values.

Difficulties of the same kind confront us in clarifying the meaning of 'the patient's best interests'. Who determines where the best interests of patients lie? In the traditional concept of medicine, this constituted no problem at all: the patient is the passive recipient of medicine, the physician is authoritative and authoritarian and knows what is best. However, the physician–patient relationship has been transformed in our time. We have come to view patients as free agents; medical paternalism is no longer accepted as the leading principle.

If medicine is defined as a specific relationship between doctor and patient, and if moral principles arise from the nature and goal of medicine, two moral principles are essential in contemporary medical ethics: the principle of respect for autonomy, and the principle of beneficence.

Philosophers such as Veatch (1979) have emphasized the idea of patient self-determination as an antidote to traditional medical paternalism. They have proposed a contractual model of health care delivery, based on the equality of the contracting parties. Each party is independent and capable of making a free and rational decision. The patient himself therefore determines what are his best interests. From this model of the healing relationship, it follows that the sole fundamental principle in medical ethics is that of respect for autonomy. It requires the physician to respect patients as self-governing in matters of their choice and actions regarding medical care. Many ethicists tend to assume that if someone is acting autonomously, then his choices morally should not be overriden by other considerations.

Others, such as Thomasma (1983b, 1984a, 1984c) object to the central role of this principle and underline the limitations of the autonomy model in health care. They point out that the concept of autonomy is not applicable to patients because illness impedes all of the features of self-determination. Personal autonomy is limited by disease. Further, the concept of autonomy assumes that the person is a relatively isolated individual essentially independent of his relations to others and to society, thereby neglecting the extent to which autonomy is a socio-cultural product.

These problems in the patient autonomy model make the principle of beneficence more attractive. It requires us to provide benefits as well as to prevent and reduce harms to others. This principle is derived internally from the healing relationship between doctor and patient which was discussed above. Beneficence, as the primary principle of medicine, claims that the physician's central task is acting in the patient's best interest, thereby overriding other principles such as patient autonomy. What the good or interest to be promoted is should be determined as a result of constant dialogue and negotiation with patients. Benefits of medical intervention must be weighed against risks of harms by disease and by interventions themselves. If the physician's and the patient's assessments do not concur, the principle of beneficence requires the physician to act in accordance with the ends of medicine. However, as we have seen health is not an objective state, but is itself a negotiable good, that is, its interpretation is negotiated between doctor and patient in the doctor–patient relationship.

Thus, from the medical perspective two moral principles are fundamental in medical ethics. These principles often come into conflict, but usually the principle of beneficence is overriding since it takes into account better the fact of illness and the nature of medicine.

The perspective of economics

Not being an economist myself, it is quite hazardous to say anything about the economic point of view. However, I have tried to derive from the relevant literature what seem to be the main features of this perspective, in order to have a clear view of the moral principles advocated by health economists.

The perspective is determined by three kinds of presuppositions: about the world, about humans, and about the nature of economics as a science.

The presuppositions about the world are summarized by Fuchs (1974). First, there is the factor of scarcity in relation to human wants. Second, resources have alternative uses; they can be used to satisfy many different wants and these wants vary in the importance attached to them.

In trying to explain human behaviour, economists make assumptions about human nature. They assume that all individuals are maximizing utility for themselves. *Homo economicus* seeks to maximize his own welfare regardless of how this compares with the welfare of others. He is pursuing a policy which he hopes will obtain the most that is possible of what he wants and the least of what he does not want. He is a perfect calculator—through and through a rational agent. Rationality in this context means the consistent pursuit of self-interest working out the most suitable means to given ends as set by a desire based on the goal of trying to ensure his own preferences are maximally benefited at minimal costs. Human rationality therefore is equated with self-interest.[11]

Since resources are scarce relative to wants, choices are inevitable. Consequently the basic problem of economics is how to allocate scarce resources so as to satisfy human wants best. Economists are 'the guardians of rationality'; economics is 'the science of choice'. As one of the social sciences, economics is the study of the allocation of scarce resources among competing wants. It provides insights concerning the distribution of goods and services as well as the consequences of different distributions. Since desire is revealed in behaviour, it examines the multiplicity of human wants and the diversity of individual preferences, by equating what people try to obtain with what they want. By virtue of these empirical and objective studies the choices that individuals and society face can be made explicit.

In the context of medicine, health is regarded as an objective of choice too (Fuchs 1976). Health care is taken as a commodity in the sense that the costs of production and consumption are measurable in terms of money, or otherwise quantifiable. Health economics is not primarily concerned with individual behaviour or well-being, but is focused on systems and particularly the institutional level of health care delivery, its priorities and objectives. At this level the individual figures as a hypostatized one (or 'aggregate citizen's sovereignty'). Individual persons are interchangeable. Health economists (or in fact health-*planning* economists) are also not accountable to individual physicians or individual patients.

The proper end of economics in this context should be promoting the cause of efficiency in health care, or in other words to ensure a more efficient health care system (Mooney 1980; McGuire and Mooney 1984). Health economists advocate the introduction of the cost–benefit approach into the health care sector, in order to measure medical performance in terms of efficiency.

However, the notion of efficiency is a difficult one. It seems to be the primary value in health economics. It is not an intrinsic value; rather it is a means towards an end outside the proper domain of economics. In this particular case health is presupposed as the fundamental value; efficiency is extrinsically valuable as that which promotes health by maximizing benefits and minimizing harms. Health economists, however, are not so much preoccupied with promoting the health of one particular patient (as is the preoccupation of a physician) as with maximizing the health of the community at large. Even if efficiency itself cannot be regarded as a moral principle, the decision on how much weight is to be given to the fact that the health care system satisfies the economic notion of efficiency is not a morally neutral decision.

Because of the existence of scarcity as well as the nature and goal of economics, the important moral principles from an economic point of view are distributive ones (de Jong and Rutten 1983). However, there are several principles that determine how burdens and benefits ought to be allocated. All these principles proceed from one formal principle: equals ought to be treated equally and unequals should be treated unequally. But we can not deduce from this elementary principle what we ought to do in a specific situation. We need an indication of what is to be regarded as equal, stating which particular respects are relevant for purposes of comparing individuals. Dependent on the context in which a principle of distribution has to be applied, we invoke a specific material principle of allocation. At least four criteria are proposed, each identifying a relevant property as the basis for distribution: equality, individual need, merit (past contribution), social worth (future contribution). The corresponding principles are systematized in ethical theories: egalitarianism (allocation of goods and services in precisely equal shares, regardless of need), Marxist theories (requiring allocation according to need), libertarianism (requiring that one is entitled to have and to keep whatever one acquires by a fair process, thus emphasizing rights to social and economic liberty and invoking criteria of contribution and merit), and utilitarianism (emphasising a mixture of criteria). Utilitarian theories are the most popular in the health economics literature. The principle of utility catches the economist's eye as the moral correlate of the notion of efficiency: maximizing the surplus of benefits over costs is morally required as well as most efficient.

3.6. Conclusion: not incompatibility but categorical diverseness

Medical and economic perspectives create a predilection for various moral principles. These principles can easily come into conflict. The question is how to handle them: are they unsolvable because the principles are essentially incompatible or is there a solution through combining the principles in a synthesis involving a renovated health care ethics as a product?

I believe that this question creates a dilemma which is false. It is assumed that what is true on the level of institutional and societal interactions is also true on the level of the transactions between concrete individuals.

The category distinction which is involved here can be illustrated from the well-known debate on the value of medicine. Modern critics such as Illich (1976) and Kennedy (1981) blame medicine for having taken the wrong path, deleterious to the health of the population. Arguing that the reduction of death from infectious diseases since the eighteenth century was due essentially to improvements in nutrition, housing, and hygiene, they conclude that the achievements of modern medicine have been overestimated and that the health status of the population can be improved more by political action and educational intervention than by medical care and medical intervention.

However, even if politics and education were successful in the prevention of disease, it is difficult to believe that they would remove the need for personal care. If better social conditions would have led to a substantial decline in the mortality rate of tuberculosis, then we cannot conclude that the provision of medical care and drugs are ineffective or unnecessary for individuals once they get tuberculosis. The care of the sick will remain the essence of the day-to-day work of the physician.

On the other hand, such criticisms draw attention to the fact that the main determinants of health lie outside the personal care system. For futher advances in health we must look to measures that change our behaviour and conditions of life.

What is important here is the distinction between the two levels of arguing, defined by McKeown (1979) as medicine as an institution and medicine as clinical practice. The diagnosis and treatment of diseases in individual patients are the objects of clinical practice. But the doctor who treats sick people cannot be expected, as McKeown points out, to deal with national food policies, changes in the environment and social attempts to modify behaviour.

The same kind of distinction is useful for elucidating the conflict between medicine and economics. Health economists are focused on the public interest; their arguments and interventions are valid at the level of medicine (or better, health care) as an institution. The arguments and interventions of doctors are focused on the private interests of individual patients, and consequently are situated at the level of clinical practice. Both levels have a different point of impact, but are nevertheless not unrelated. Their relationship can be specified as one of subordination rather than co-ordination.

Health care as an institution constitutes the framework within which health care as clinical practice is operating. This subordination is clear in the case of allocative decisions. Macro-allocation determines *whether* to allocate resources for the development or production of, say, a new technology, whereas micro-allocation determines *how* to allocate the technology to individuals once it is available. 'First-order determinations' on the institutional level settle the scope of individual possibilities.[12] The same same subordination obtains in my opinion with ethical questions. We cannot in medical ethics have at the same time a great concern for social welfare as well as for individual welfare. *Medical* ethics necessarily is concerned with the individual good. But it can only function within a more encompassing *health care* ethics which is primarily concerned with the common good.

The key issue in ethical disputes is to analyse the relationship between the common good and the good of individuals, particularly the extent to which the common good ought to be concurrent with the individual good.

Notes

1. Bullough (1966) describes how medicine had actually emerged as a profession by the sixteenth century and he terminates his book at that time. Chapman (1979) draws attention to the fact that the Royal College of Physicians of London in 1563 applied the adjective 'ethical' (replacing the label 'penal') to its organizational statutes. In doing so the College was setting a precedent because Thomas Percival, and via his code American Medical Societies, adopted this specific use of the terms 'ethical' and 'medical ethics'.
2. In the opinion of Chapman (1979), ethical codes represent organizational rules and regulations, whereas the profession's basic ethical principle is not put into written form. The unwritten patient-centred ethic might read in his words: 'Once the professional relation between physician and patient is established, the physician must put the patient's interests, welfare and rights above all other considerations' (*op. cit.* p. 632).
3. This view of ethics is not explicitly propounded in Mooney (1980), but it is evidently presupposed.
4. This metaphor is introduced by Mooney (1983): medical ethics as a two-legged stool (i.e. individualistic ethics of virtue and duty).
5. I do not agree with Beauchamp and Childress (1983) that this weakness of

professional codes may be outweighed by their value in controlling moral conduct. See Warnock (1971) for a critique of the misconceived analogy of moral rules and legal rules.

6. This statement implies two things: (i) Professional norms are not independent of ordinary norms (i.e. norms that apply to everyone); so the claim of ethical relativism is not accepted; (ii) the accepted values of society themselves have to be justifiable: 'At a higher lever, a complete justification of professional ethics involves the justification of societal values' (Bayles 1981, p. 20).

7. The importance of rules in moral philosophy is questioned by Warnock (1971). He suggested that '. . . to hold moral views . . . is not to be thought of as "recognizing" or "accepting" a system of rules, but rather as recognizing some range or variety of reasons for judging and, when appropriate, for saying or doing' (*op. cit.* p. 70). Consequently, the notion of 'moral reasons' is fundamental. A moral reason is 'a consideration, about some person, or some person's character, or some specimen of actual or possible conduct, which tends to establish in the subject concerned conformity or conflict with a moral principle' (*op. cit.* p. 86).

8. See for instance Baier (1958) and Warnock (1967, 1971). 'In ethical reasoning about a particular case there is never any guarantee, but there is always some hope, given that each will try to understand the other's arguments' (Walton 1982, p. 123).

9. 'There is, therefore, a special dimension of anguish in illness. That is why healing cannot be classified as a commodity . . .' (Pellegrino 1979, p. 45).

   Asymmetry in information between doctor and patient is not as important in health care, as Mooney (1983, p. 6) supposes. The physician–patient relationship has some elements of the supplier–consumer relationship (e.g. inequality of knowledge and skill), but is essentially different from it: 'What is different is the unique ontological assault of illness on the body–self unity, and the primacy of the freedom to deal with all other life situations which illness removed' (Pellegrino, *op.cit.* p. 45).

10. See for instance, Cassell (1976, 1982), Engelhardt (1982), Thomasma (1984b), Kass (1975).

11. Personal choice and personal welfare cannot be identified, as Sen (1977) pointed out. The notion of rationality as the maximization of utility is criticized on various grounds, for example a rational course of action (in this sense) cannot be relied on to produce the best results; internal consistency is not enough to assure rationality; this conception of rationality makes it impossible to explain why individuals should have a preference for the welfare of others (in fact it is irrational to contribute to the public good unless it pays to the individual; so rationality also assumes individualism, i.e. the community is nothing more than the combination of its members). See Trigg (1985) and Rescher (1980).

12. 'First-order determinations define the global setting, whether existentially imposed, as in a condition of absolute natural scarcity, or, as is the more common case, one chosen on the basis of relative priorities within the larger context of ultimate natural scarcities, for instance, a population-restrictive policy which sets acceptable rates of procreation in a society. Second-order determinations allocate the available resources as defined by the first order, for instance, who may have children, how many, when, and so forth' (Calabresi and Bobbitt 1978, p. 19).

38   *Henk ten Have*

References

Arend, A. van der (1987). Normative aspects of professionalization in nursing. In Carmi, A. (ed.) *Ethics and law in nursing* **II**. Springer Verlag, Berlin (in press).

Baier, K. (1958). *The moral point of view*. Cornell University Press, Ithaca.

Ballantine, H. T. (1979). The crisis in ethics, anno domini 1979. *New England Journal of Medicine* **301**, 634–8.

Bayles, M. D. (1981). *Professional ethics*. Wadsworth, Belmont.

Beauchamp, T. L. and Childress, J. F. (1983). *Principles of biomedical ethics*. (2nd edition). Oxford University Press. New York/Oxford.

Beauchamp, T. L. and McCullough, L. B. (1984). *Medical ethics. The moral responsibilities of physicians*. Prentice-Hall, Englewood Cliffs.

Bullough, V. L. (1966). *The development of medicine as a profession*. Karger, Basel/New York.

Calabresi, G. and Bobbitt, P. (1978). *Tragic choices*. Norton & Comp., New York.

Cassell, E. J. (1976). *The healer's art. A new approach to the doctor–patient relationship*. Lippincott, Philadelphia and New York.

Cassell, E. J. (1982). The nature of suffering and the goals of medicine. *New England Journal of Medicine* **306**, 639–45.

Chapman, C. B. (1979). On the definition and teaching of the medical ethic. *New England Journal of Medicine* **301**, 630–4.

Downie, R. S. (1974). *Roles and values. An introduction to social ethics*. Methuen, London.

Engelhardt, H. T. (1982). Goals of medicine. A reappraisal. In Bell, N. K. (ed.) *Who decides? Conflicts of rights in health care*. pp. 49–66. Humana Press, Clifton.

Fox, D. M. (1979). The segregation of medical ethics: a problem in modern intellectual history. *The Journal of Medicine and Philosophy* **4**, 81–97.

Fuchs, V. R. (1974). *Who shall live? Health, economics, and social choice*. Basic Books, New York.

Fuchs, V. R. (1976). Concepts of health—an economist's perspective. *Journal of Medicine and Philosophy* **1**, 229–37.

Harron, F., Burnside, J. and Beauchamp, T. (1983). *Health and human values*. Yale University Press, New Haven and London.

Have, H. ten and Arend, A. van der (1985). Philosophy of medicine in the Netherlands. *Theoretical Medicine* **6**, 1–42.

Illich, I. (1976). *Limits to medicine*. Penguin Books, Harmondsworth.

Jong, G. A. de and Rutten, F. F. H. (1983). Justice and health for all. *Social Science and Medicine* **17**, 1085–95.

Kass, L. R. (1975). Regarding the end of medicine and the pursuit of health. *Public Interest* **40**, 11–42.

Kennedy, I. (1981). *The unmasking of medicine*. Allen and Unwin, London.

McGuire, A. and Mooney, G. (1985). *Ethics and property rights in the NHS hospital*. Health Economics Research Unit Discussion paper no. 02/85, University of Aberdeen.

MacIntyre, A. (1981). *After virtue. A study in moral theory*. Duckworth, London.

McKeown, T. (1979). *The role of medicine. Dream, mirage or nemesis?* (2nd edition). Blackwell, Oxford.

Mooney, G. H. (1980). Cost–benefit analysis and medical ethics. *Journal of medical ethics* 6, 177–9.

Mooney, G. (1983). *Are medical ethics and economics incompatible?* Health Economics Research Unit, Discussion paper no. 3/83, University of Aberdeen, 1983.

Pellegrino, E. D. (1979). Toward a reconstruction of medical morality: the primacy of the act of profession and the fact of illness. *Journal of Medicine and Philosophy* 4, 32–56.

Pellegrino, E. D. and Thomasma, D. C. (1981). *A philosophical basis of medical practice. Toward a philosophy and ethic of the healing profession*. Oxford University Press, New York/Oxford.

Rescher, N. (1980). *Unpopular essays on technological progress*. University of Pittsburgh Press, Pittsburgh.

Sen, A. (1977). Rational fools: a critique of the behavioural foundations of economic theory. *Philosophy and Public Affairs* 6, 317–44.

Thomasma, D. C. (1983a). The role of the clinical medical ethicist: the problem of applied ethics and medicine. In Bradie, M., Attig, T. W. and Rescher, N. (eds.) *The applied turn in contemporary philosophy*. Bowling Green Studies in applied philosophy 5, 136–57.

Thomasma, D. C. (1983b). Limitations of the autonomy model for the doctor–patient relationship. *The Pharos of Alpha Omega Alpha* 46, 2–5.

Thomasma, D. C. (1984a). What does medicine contribute to ethics? *Theoretical Medicine* 5, 267–77.

Thomasma, D. C. (1984b). The goals of medicine and society. In Brock, D. H. (ed.) *The culture of biomedicine* pp. 34–54. Associated University Presses, London and Toronto.

Thomasma, D. C. (1984c). Autonomy in the doctor–patient relation. *Theoretical Medicine* 5, 1–7.

Trigg, R. (1985). *Understanding social science. A philosophical introduction to the social sciences*. Blackwell, Oxford.

Veatch, R. M. (1979). Professional medical ethics: the grounding of its principles. *Journal of Medicine and Philosophy* 4, 1–19.

Walton, D. W. (1982). Comments on a medical ethics for the future: a commentary on Andre de Vries. *Metamedicine* 3, 121–4.

Warnock, G. J. (1967). *Contemporary moral philosophy*. Macmillan, London.

Warnock, G. J. (1971). *The object of morality*. Methuen, London.

Williams, A. (1985). *Medical ethics, health service efficiency and clinical freedom*. Nuffield/York Portfolios, Folio 2, Nuffield Provincial Hospitals Trust, London.

4

Traditional medical ethics and economics in health care: a critique

R. S. DOWNIE

Summary

*There is a sharp distinction traditionally drawn between 'the profes-
sions' and other occupations. This distinction can seem especially
striking if we look at the doctor–patient relationship in market terms;
the market weakness of the patient as consumer seems to require a
special medical ethics to offer protection. On closer examination, the
commodity of health care, and the doctor–patient relationship which
delivers it, are less different from standard market relationships than
has been traditionally thought, and the case for a special medical
ethics therefore weakens. The moral duties of medicine are best seen
as correlative to the needs and rights of patients. The individualism
necessarily built in to the doctor–patient relationship requires to be
supplemented by social ethics and economics, but it does not follow
that such social ethics needs to be utilitarian.*

Coleridge (1817) tells us that the object of Wordsworth's poetry was 'to
give the charm of novelty to things of every day' and 'to remove the film of
familiarity' which covers our perception of ordinary situations, objects and
people. For example, in his long poem *The Prelude* Wordsworth describes
a chance meeting with an old soldier, but the meeting takes place in a
lonely road in the moonlight. The effect of this is to remove for us the
familiarity with which we view each other in everyday life. Wordsworth
succeeds in bringing out the essential strangeness and loneliness of human
beings and their lives.

Now I do not think that Mooney and McGuire (Chapter 2) would be
altogether flattered by the comparison if I am taken to be suggesting that
their description of the doctor–patient relationship in the language of
economics was putting it into the moonlight! I am really saying that it is
beneficial to come to see a familiar relationship in an unfamiliar way.
Traditionally, we have been encouraged by the medical profession to see
doctors as motivated by especially high ideals called 'medical ethics'.
Indeed, one writer on professional ethics sees the professions as 'the

conscience of society' (Sieghart 1985). It puts the whole doctor–patient relationship in a new light therefore when Mooney and McGuire invite us to see it in terms of economic concepts, and it emerges that Santa Claus is only Uncle Jim! But, granted that it is refreshing to see a familiar relationship described in an unfamiliar way, is the description at the end of the day sound? I shall begin by looking at the main points in their interesting argument.

1. The health care sector can be seen in terms of the concepts of a market, but it differs from other economic structures, especially in that the doctor is performing on both sides of the market. He both acts as an agent for the patient in the process of the demand for treatment, and specifies the supply of treatment.
2. The potential abuses of this situation are to some extent remedied in that the doctor is constrained by medical ethics.
3. But medical ethics is individualistic and therefore not well adapted to fill the utilitarian requirement of an economically efficient system of health care. Medical ethics should therefore be supplemented by social ethics which is the concern of the citizens rather than the doctor.
4. This supplementary social ethics should be founded on utilitarianism.

These propositions provide a framework for a worthwhile moral, political, and economic discussion. Some of the important critical points are made by ten Have (Chapter 3) and I shall make use of them in my own discussion. I shall begin this with an examination of the first proposition, which is the foundation of the whole Mooney–McGuire argument—the analysis of the doctor–patient relationship in economic terms.

4.1.   The market and the doctor–patient relationship

The classic account of the market, to which Mooney and McGuire subscribe, attributes to a market, or to an economic relationship between people, at least the following characteristics:

1. The trading parties are each attempting to maximize their own self-interests (nowadays called by economists 'utility functions').
2. They have information to guide them on this.
3. The parties are free to choose whether they will trade or not.
4. The consumer and the producer each bear their own costs.
5. The relationship is a competitive one in a double sense: producers or suppliers are competing with consumers to maximize their profits and producers are competing with other producers to attract consumers.
6. There must be a legal framework to ensure fair competition.

It is not surprising that Mooney and McGuire find that the doctor–patient relationship does not fit easily into this pattern. The patient is lacking in information, and so his choice of treatment is restricted. For other reasons his choice of doctor may be restricted. Indeed, since the doctor supplies the information to the patient he largely determines the patient's choice. He also supplies the treatment and evaluates its success. The costs are borne neither by the doctor nor the patient, although this depends on the system of health care, but by some third party such as the state or an insurance company. *If* this is an accurate description of the situation then certainly a patient is in a vulnerable position. To some extent of course, the patient can be protected by a legal framework, but more protection is needed than law provides, and hence medical ethics, as traditionally understood, has developed to defend the patient.

A criticism of this picture might try to show either that the traditional economist's account of a free market is misleading, or that the consequential account of the doctor–patient relationship is misleading. In the remainder of this section and in the next, I shall try to show that both are misleading, and that the role traditionally played by medical ethics is not the one suggested by Mooney and McGuire. I shall then suggest another way of looking at medical ethics.

The central assumption in the Mooney–McGuire position on the nature of a market is the one derived from Adam Smith (1776)—that self-interest is the basis of the market, or that consumers will always strive to maximize their utility. There are many passages in the *Wealth of Nations* which assume or assert this but the best known is the following:

In almost every other race of animals, each individual, when it is grown up to maturity, is entirely independent, and in the natural state has occasion for the assistance of no other living creature. But man has almost constant occasion for the help of his brethern, and it is in vain for him to expect it from their benevolence only. He is more likely to prevail if he can interest their self-love in his favour, and show them that it is to their own advantage to do for him what he requires of them . . . It is not from the benevolence of the butcher, the brewer, or the baker that we expect our dinner, but from their regard to their own self-interest. We address ourselves, not to their humanity, but to their self-love, and never talk to them of our own necessities, but of their advantages.

This is a persuasive passage, but I believe that it is in important ways confused and I shall try to expose some of the complexities which lie beneath the surface rhetoric.

Is Adam Smith correct in claiming that the butcher (or any trader) serves us out of self-interest rather than benevolence? The answer depends on whether we interpret the claim as an empirical or as a conceptual one. Interpreted as an empirical generalization, about the reason for which actual traders act on specific occasions, it certainly cannot be known to be true since it is notoriously difficult to know what people's motives really are, and it may in fact be contingently false, since some traders may well on some occasions act out of benevolence, at least in the sense of a desire to provide a service to their customers. Many butchers and other traders may pride themselves in their skilled crafts and find satisfaction, for example, in educating customers in the best cuts of meat for certain purposes, how to cook them, and so on. More plausibly interpreted in conceptual terms, or in terms of what Max Weber calls an 'ideal type', the claim concerns the motive of the butcher *qua* butcher, and it is to the effect that, whatever the actual motives, if any, of Mr X and Mr Y who happen to be butchers, the motive of butchers as such is necessarily self-interest in the form of the maximum profit obtainable. But in reply we should note that it is false—this time necessarily false—that the butcher *qua* butcher is aiming at maximum profit. Rather, the defining aim of the butcher is the carving, mincing, and otherwise dispensing of meat, and a good butcher is one who does these things well, not necessarily one who makes a profit. In a similar way, the doctor *qua* doctor aims at curing or treating his patients, and one doctor is better than another in respect of his skill in attaining this end, rather than that of high fees.

It might be objected that a trader is also a business man, and as such must make a profit. But while this is true it says nothing peculiar to the market, for the professional man also must make a profit in the form of his fee or salary, and so must anyone who earns his living. Distinctions of this kind which are blurred in much thinking since Adam Smith, are made explicitly in Greek thought. It seems to me, then, that the claim that self-interest is the basis of the market is on one interpretation contingently false, on another necessarily false, and on a third trivially true.

This suggests that the doctor and the patient are not so very unlike the producer and the consumer with respect to (1), the central assumption of the free market; the difference, if any, is mainly one of emphasis, or even just in the use of terms like 'profit', rather than 'fee' or 'salary'. But what of the other conditions of the market? Take (2), the flow of information. It is true that if we contrast, say, being a consumer of apples in a free market with being a consumer of chemotherapy there seems to be a contrast, in that most people know what sort of apples they want and whether they are good apples or not, whereas few people have the same sort of information about chemotherapy. But the contrast here is at its starkest. Let us suppose that an average motorist is advised by his garage mechanic that his engine needs some expensive treatment, or that a philosopher wishes to purchase a word processor. There is a similar lack of information here too. True, the motorist can ask friends for their advice on garages and the philosopher can ask colleagues about word processors. But the patient too can ask others. There are many health magazines, TV programmes, and nurses who can advise. Moreover, a patient can also ask for a 'second opinion'. Hence, unless the patient is unconscious, the situations are not so very different; or rather, there is a continuum. At one end the information is technical and the consumer depends on the producer to act as his agent in the supply of information, and at the other the consumer can find out adequately for himself. But both medical and other goods and services are equally spread out along this continuum.

The same is true of (3) choice. In the medical situation choices are often forced on a patient by circumstances, but so also if one's car has broken down may choices be forced on us. The financing of medicine (4) does seem to be different in its operation from commerce, at least in the modern world, in that finances come from third parties. But this is by no means unique to medicine. Compare education: in state education the financing is by third parties. Competition (5) is less prevalent in health care because of its monopolistic nature. But it is possible to change one's doctor or dentist, and this is not a matter of indifference to these professions since there can be financial implications. Legal frameworks (6) apply to both medicine and commerce alike and indeed the law is taking a much greater part as a watchdog than formerly, especially in the USA.

The conclusion suggested by this is not that the traditional picture of economic relationships in a free market is completely inaccurate, but just that it is oversimplified, and that when some of the complications are added the contrast between the producer–consumer relationship and the doctor–patient relationship is not so marked. Indeed, in a more detailed study it would be interesting to examine the extent to which market features are found in medicine, such as fashions in treatments or operations, the use of doctors as agents of insurance companies, the existence of commercial 'off the street' sterilization services and many others. For present purposes, however, I wish to insist merely on a milder thesis, that the traditional contrast between commerce on the one hand and 'the professions' on the other seems to be exaggerated.

4.2. Traditional medical ethics, safeguards, and ordinary morality

Turning now to the second proposition in the Mooney and McGuire analysis—that medical ethics provides at least some safeguard for the patient, granted his vulnerability—I wish to assert that medical ethics as traditionally understood has been useless as a safeguard, or even harmful through its effects on medical attitudes to patients. Indeed, I should be willing to generalize this claim and assert that the whole conception of professional ethics has done more harm than good, although I shall not argue the more general thesis here.

Note, to begin with, that I am speaking of medical ethics 'as traditionally understood'. I believe that this is how Mooney and McGuire are conceiving medical ethics. In the concepts of Henk ten Have, Mooney and McGuire are depicting medical ethics as a 'product'; in other words, as a set of formulae which have been codified and can be distributed in a handbook.

Ten Have has given an excellent brief critique of codes so understood and Sohl (Chapter 6) has added historical information on the development of codes, but I should like to add some criticisms from the point of view of my own argument.

The most famous code—the Hippocratic Oath—sets the example of a code of medical ethics which is still followed. In the Hippocratic Oath there are two main elements. First, there are some inward-looking rules concerned with respecting teachers and caring for their families without charge, passing on knowledge to pupils, and not trespassing on the patch of colleagues in related areas of knowledge (as Hippocrates suggests that physicians should not attempt to cut for the stone but should leave cutting to those trained in that line). These are the rules one expects to find in any sort of fraternity; they show an aspect of professional concern which may be perfectly proper but is hardly an expression of moral idealism.

The second main ingredient in a code of medical or other professional ethics is much more important from the moral point of view. It consists of some generalized exhortations to care for patients, which can be summed up by saying that the medical and perhaps all the professions are governed to a much greater extent than other jobs by the principle of benevolence. Indeed Gillon (1986) goes so far as to describe the doctor's duty as one of *supererogatory* benevolence, in that it goes beyond what can reasonably be expected of the rest of us.

A short way to dispose of this claim might be to argue that it confuses conceptual points about the definition of the aims of a profession with moral duties; definitional 'oughts' have been confused with moral 'oughts'. Thus, it sounds like a high ideal to say that the doctor ought to care for the health or the welfare of his patient, but in fact this is simply a definition of the job of a doctor. The shepherd *qua* shepherd ought to care for his sheep, the gardener *qua* gardener ought to care for his flower beds and grass, and the pilot *qua* pilot ought to aim at transporting his passengers with safety. These are just definitions of occupations in terms of their aims. Of course, one might say that the person who happens to be a doctor ought to do the best he can as a doctor. Yes, and the person who happens to be a gardener ought to do the best he can for his flower beds. We all ought to work hard in our respective spheres. In other words, if medical ethics is made to seem grander than ordinary morality it is because a conceptual claim has become confused with a perfectly ordinary moral claim.

An argument of this kind is usually thought by doctors to be too superficial. They reply that patients are vulnerable and that health care must be delivered through the uniquely special doctor–patient relationship. But that uniquely special relationship requires a special morality to protect it, and so we need medical ethics as traditionally understood.

Yet what is uniquely special about the doctor–patient relationship? What emerges after any attempt to answer this question is that it is difficult to find a set of necessary and sufficient conditions, which justify the description 'uniquely special' of the doctor–patient relationship. Note to begin with that there is no one relationship which is *the* doctor/patient relationship. For example, an anaesthetist might see a patient once before an operation, but adding this to the anaesthetist's function during an operation hardly creates a 'relationship', and in any case it is certainly different from the 'relationship' which a community health doctor might have with the population who live in a given geographical area. But even waiving this objection and concentrating on certain typical sorts of doctor–patient relationships we cannot easily say what is uniquely special about them. Certainly, patients are lacking in information and power when, say, a coronary artery bypass operation is prescribed, but so are most of us when the garage mechanic prescribes an engine transplant! In each case most of us must trust in the knowledge, skills, and good faith of our helpers. Perhaps car engines are not so important as our bodies, but then we also commit the latter to the care of airline pilots and taxi drivers. Again, doctors may have access to our bodies; but teachers, clergymen, and advertisers have access to our minds and can influence to varying degrees our very perceptions of our own identities. The conclusion seems to be that if there are *uniquely* defining conditions of the doctor–patient relationship they are likely to be trivial and not special in the sense of important, and if there are special or important features they are likely to be shared with a variety of occupations such as the lifeboat service, the police, the clergy, teachers, and many others, some of which are 'professions' and some not. It seems more profitable then to drop the whole idea of uniquely special features of the doctor–patient relationship and to draw attention to 'family resemblances' between that relationship and a whole variety of others.

To argue, as I have done, that there is nothing uniquely special about the doctor–patient relationship certainly weakens the claim that there is a need for a special sort of morality. But it does not dispose of it entirely. I wish now to argue that medical ethics as traditionally understood is actually harmful to health care, and that the need is really to drop the traditional approach and to re-assert the claims of ordinary morality (Downie and Calman 1987).

The first respect in which traditional medical ethics has been harmful to health care concerns the distortions it has created in the doctor–patient relationship. For example, traditional codes are expressed in terms of the duties of the doctor, and while this has certainly inspired an idealistic practice it has also created a professional ethos of elitism and paternalism. Thus, generations of medical students have been given the impression that there is an esoteric set of rules—'medical ethics'—which govern their professional activities. It is easy to extrapolate from this to the conclusion that such a code is different from and superior to ordinary morality. Doctors are not as other men; other men are guided by right and wrong, but doctors have medical ethics. For example, in ordinary life the assumption, if not the reality, is that people speak the truth to each other, but this is not an assumption of those governed by medical ethics; for medical ethics says that the first responsibility of the doctor is to the well-being of his patient, and it is generally thought to follow that it is up to the doctor to decide how far, in his opinion, a patient's well-being will be furthered by telling the truth. Medical ethics in this respect distorts the doctor–patient relationship, for any true human relationship must have sincerity as its necessary condition, and that condition is discouraged by the attitude built into traditional medical ethics: benevolence (if that is what it is) has swamped sincerity. This criticism might be summed up by saying that the duties of doctors should not be regarded, as they are in the tradition, as duties of benevolence, but rather as duties correlative to the *rights of patients*. To give this emphasis to the doctor–patient relationship is to cut out the distortion caused by the tradition. Indeed, an emphasis on rights—consumer rights, social and political rights, human rights of all kinds—is one moral characteristic of our time. This point is developed by Roscam-Abbing (Chapter 5).

A second criticism which can be made of the tradition is that its fraternal, inward-looking nature discourages frank and open co-operation with other caring professions. For example, nurses and social workers are not part of the fraternity so it has been a matter for debate how far they should be admitted into the inner counsels. One consequence of this is inefficiency in the delivery of health care due to uncertainty or lack of co-operation among all the members of a health care team. Where objectives are not shared and discussed among the caring professions there is a diminution of job satisfaction, friction, and a consequent damage to patient care. For example, one member of a team, a nurse, say, may not know how much a patient has been told or what the overall prognosis is. It is then difficult for the nurse to be fully supportive of the patient. This is not good morality.

A third respect in which the traditional approach to medical ethics is deficient is that it suggests that morality is about selected issues, rather than that it is all-pervasive. The discussion of medical ethics has tended to highlight the dramatic issues which happen to be topical at any one time. Although euthanasia, abortion, resuscitation, surrogate motherhood, and human experimentation are undoubtedly important matters, their promi-

nence has obscured the fact that, not just once but many times in the course
of a working day, moral stances, value judgements, and decisions will result
in actions considered to be right or wrong by the doctor. This is partly, but
only partly, due to the uncertain nature of medical diagnosis and prognosis.
The doctor, lacking certainty, must estimate what in his opinion is for the
total good of the patient. This concept of 'total good' is not just a matter of
technical expertise but involves values. For example, let us imagine a
70-year-old man who wants to be allowed home soon after an operation.
The doctor's judgement here will involve technical expertise, but will also
involve economic and value judgements of a total good, including knowledge of the home circumstances and many other factors. Again, whether
we do a job only moderately well when we are capable of doing it better is
a question of morality, of deciding which direction we want to take.
Allowing ourselves to become professionally socialized into routinized
working patterns which keep things going but diminish patients' dignity
and freedom requires as much a moral justification as a sociological
explanation. These moral demands are all-pervasive and inescapable in
health care.

Fourth, the traditional distinction between 'medical ethics' and 'private
morality' suggests that one can deal with moral questions in a professional
context without examining personal values and convictions. But I am
arguing that it follows from the inescapable and all-pervasive nature of
morality that we encounter moral problems in our personal lives which are
not fundamentally different from those we may have to explore in our
working environment. Whatever values we may feel to be important to us
as individuals are almost certainly influencing and directing the decisions
that we make as professional health care workers. If we have or lack the
skills which allow us to approach moral dilemmas in a rational and
methodical way in ordinary life, this will affect how we attempt to solve
moral problems in a professional context. In other words, morality is
'indivisible'.

On the other hand, this fundamental assumption about the 'indivisibility'
of morality does not lead to a rejection of the very special place that the
maintence of acceptable professional standards of behaviour must have in
the work of people whose primary responsibility is to care for vulnerable
fellow men and women. The potential harm that can come to people who
are in some ways and by definition dependent on the knowledge and skills
of others will undoubtedly heighten the moral concern in situations which,
outside the professional context, might not be perceived as quite so
threatening or acute. For example, a critical or sarcastic remark, which
might be acceptable in ordinary circumstances, could be devastating to a
sick person.

Another aspect of the 'indivisibility' of morality is that hospitals and other health care organizations ought not to be immune to general attitudinal changes in society. Moral dilemmas arise frequently from the attempts which the professions make or do not make to accommodate social change. Likewise, what professional people do, or often more pertinently what they would refuse to do, reflects the moral standards of their society in the same way in which actions of the individual doctor or nurse, psychologist or speech therapist, social worker or dietician reflect his or her standards of personal morality. The dilemmas created by social change can be obscured by an emphasis on medical ethics traditionally understood as a product.

A fifth criticism of traditional medical ethics is that it tends to underestimate the fact that medical decisions ought to be made in the real world of technological and economic facts. This point is much stressed in the papers of Mooney and McGuire, and Jennett (Chapter 7). Traditionally, medical ethics tends to be seen in terms of pure moral absolutes—the doctor must do all that is medically possible for *his* (or her) patient regardless of the cost. I am asserting that in the real world compromises must be made. As an example of compromise we can point to renal dialysis. It is not helpful to say that there is an absolute value on human life if there are two patients who would benefit from dialysis but facilities for treating only one. The moral requirement here is to reflect on the scientific and economic facts of the cases as well as the quality of life of the potential recipients. This point can be expressed in the form of a distinction between compromising our consciences, which is wrong, and conscientious compromises, which consist in making the moral best of a bad job in the light of scientific and economic constraints. This distinction is compatible with the view that in some circumstances no compromises should be made.

These five criticisms of traditional medical ethics support Henk ten Have and suggest that an enlightened medical ethics will be in terms of a 'process'—the process of applying the principles of everyday morality to the scientific and economic complexities of patient care. Moral decisions in medicine are what can be called 'consequential' or 'resultant' in that they arise out of the professional, economic, and legal facts of given cases. Ethics is no substitute for a good diagnosis of the problem, skilfully carried out treatment or clearly communicated information, but equally in doing these things the doctor is at the same time engaging in moral and economic activity.

4.3. Individualism and economics

The third proposition of the Mooney–McGuire analysis is that medical ethics as traditionally understood is individualistic and therefore ill adapted to the utilitarian requirements of an economically efficient system of health care. If we substitute (as I have urged) the idea of ordinary morality in a medical context for medical ethics the same point could be made; ordinary morality is individualistic. How far is the Mooney–McGuire proposition acceptable?

The principle of utility tells us that we ought to produce the best possible consequences for the majority, and there is no doubt that an efficient use of resources is important in achieving this. Now the individual is certainly ill placed to work out for himself what would produce the best possible consequence for the majority, but, as J. S. Mill (1863) pointed out long ago, he can be guided in this by rules which distil the wisdom of mankind on the consequences of action. Mill is here thinking of moral rules, but there is no reason why the idea should not be extended to apply more generally to guidelines which could cover such matters as prescribing and treatment. This is not a new idea. As Gillon (Chapter 9) points out doctors do in fact take some cognisance of economic costs, and I am simply suggesting that this factor should become more explicit. GPs, for example, could be issued with budgets in terms of the size and nature of their practice with guidelines on prescribing. It would then be their decision as to how to allocate resources within that population. A just and efficient allocation of resources is possible within a manageable population such as a general practice. The details of such schemes are no doubt complex but there seems to me no doubt that Mooney–McGuire are correct in the general lines of their claim on this matter, that medical ethics, however interpreted, has an individualistic basis and should therefore be buttressed with some budgetary control. But I am maintaining that at least some budgetary control, or even awareness, is achievable within a framework of individualism.

But to encourage budgetary control at the level of the individual leaves untouched the problem of how resources should be allocated within the health sector of the economy as a whole. This, as Mooney and McGuire maintain, is more a matter of social ethics than medical ethics as traditionally understood. Henk ten Have speaks of 'health care ethics' to cover this wider area. Mooney and McGuire make the point that doctors are not qualified to take part in this debate. Now if the debate is about resources which should be allocated to health from a national budget then this is a matter for a political forum and doctors must be restricted to playing their roles in the democratic political process. If, however, the debate is more narrowly conducted and is over the allocation of resources within the total health budget then doctors must clearly be involved as well as economists and others. In this context I am thinking of questions such as the allocation of resources to geriatrics rather than to paediatrics, etc. Expert medical advice is clearly required here, but the danger is that if others are not also involved then the allocation of resources tends to go to those with the most effective medical pressure group. In other words, resources are allocated on the basis of power rather than on rational criteria. Perhaps there is scope here for 'ethical committees' at a national as well as at local level to advise on allocation.

4.4. Social ethics and utilitarianism

It is possible for a philosopher to make more of a contribution to the fourth and last of the Mooney and McGuire propositions which I shall consider—that the social ethic on which health care in this wider sense should be based must be utilitarian. The question to be addressed is this: is utilitarianism acceptable as the sole basis for an extended social ethics of health care?

The answer is that it is not, for at least two reasons. The first of these is a familar one and dates back to the beginning of the utilitarian movement. It is simply that any version of the utilitarian principle must be supplemented by a principle of justice to be at all plausible. Utilitarians have from the outset been aware of the importance of the principle of justice and have made various attempts to show how it is entailed by utility. In my opinion all these attempts have failed. The utilitarian principle is concerned with the interests of the majority, but justice is concerned with the interests of each person equally. These principles are distinct *conceptually* and irreducible the one to the other; one speaks of the *majority*, the other of *each individual equally*. Moreover, it is not true *in fact* that the interests of each individually are necessarily furthered by a policy concerned to promote majority interests. For example, it is no doubt in the interests of the majority that health care should be concentrated in large centres of population, but such a policy is manifestly unfair to those living in rural areas.

Some utilitarians would reply that the *means* whereby the majority interests are brought about is a factor in the determination of what should count as majority interests. Mooney and McGuire refer to this as 'process utility' as distinct from 'end-state utility'. For example, the argument might be that the majority do not want their interest to be furthered at the expense of the interests of the minority. No doubt this is true, but it misses the point. The point is that the interests of the minority make a moral claim *independent* of majority interests. This is logically entailed by the principle of justice, that each counts equally. The social and political debate, if it is to have a moral dimension, must not therefore be simply that of deciding how majority interests can be furthered (i.e. simply in terms of the principle of utility) but how majority interest can best be furthered consistently with giving everyone equal consideration (i.e. in terms not just of utility but also of justice or fairness). To say this is not of course to say that utility must never prevail—sometimes the minorities must go to the wall in the interests of the majority—but it is to say that no groups of individuals must go to the wall without an equal consideration of their interests. Indeed, even were it true that the interests of the majority were always furthered in fact by considering the interests of each person equally, or that the interests of each equally were furthered by considering first the interests of the majority, these contingencies would not establish the principle of utility as the sole principle—a principle of justice, fairness, or equal consideration of interests is still morally necessary. No version of utilitarianism, however sophisticated, can accommodate this point, and the 'can' is a logical one referring to the identity of the principle of utility.

The second criticism concerns the utilitarian idea of society and social good. Society for the utilitarian is simply a collective noun for the individuals who at any given moment make up society. It follows on the utilitarian analysis that the good of society or social welfare is just the aggregate goods or interests (or 'utilities') of the individuals who make up society or a given society at a given time. Moreover, the individual is conceived on the model of the consumer; to be a person for a utilitarian is just to be a consumer. But consumers do not always know what they want, or consume what is good for them. There is a hint of this criticism in Mooney and McGuire when they quote Harsanyi and Sen and Williams to the effect that people may not actually want what it is rational for them to want. In other words, we have moved from actual preferences and aggregated utilities to 'true' preferences and 'correct' policies. Implicit in this idea is something which is far removed from the utilitarian individualistic and hedonistic view of the self and the community. What we now have is a conception of the 'true' interests of the individual and presumably also the true interests of a continuing community. To illustrate this let us take a problem on the margins of health care and community medicine—the problem of environmental pollution.

If we take seriously social problems such as that of pollution, we are necessarily operating with hazy conceptions of a *public* interest and of a continuing community. The point here is not that a government may impose some conception of intrinsic good with no relation to what individuals within a society actually want, but rather that it must develop the implications of what people at a given time actually want in order to elicit an enlightened conception of what in the long run they, and their *successors*, will want. The utilitarian tradition of individualism and hedonism cannot easily accommodate the idea of the true interest of a continuing community without ceasing to be utilitarianism.

4.5 Ethics, economics, and medical education

By way of an appendix I shall consider the implications of all this for the education of a doctor. This section should be read in conjunction with

Vang's contribution (Chapter 10). (See also Downie and Calman 1987.) There is a strong case for including in a medical curriculum some lectures and discussions on health economics. Many medical courses include large amounts of medical jurisprudence, anatomy, and other traditional components which could perhaps be pruned to make way for health economics. This would not turn medical students into economists, but what it would do would be to provide an additional conceptual framework with which to view health care. There would be no difficulty in combining such a course with one on moral philosophy. Once again the emphasis should be on conceptual frameworks, on providing ways of looking at health care which remove the film of familiarity through which medical students see medicine.

But that still leaves the question of the first-order moral problem of medicine. Moral philosophy and health economics are a help here but they cannot solve such problems. Can morality itself be taught? This question was much discussed by Plato. One difficulty in teaching morality is that it is not just a matter of knowledge, or of skills (both of which can be taught), but of attitudes, and attitudes are more easily 'caught' like an infectious disease than taught. To illustrate this, consider the traditional way of teaching medical ethics, and its defects.

The traditional method—although 'method' is perhaps the wrong term since it is never fully explicit—involves two stages. In the first stage, which usually takes place early in the student's college or university years, some important and senior person will arrive and give a lecture or two on the relevant 'Code of Ethics' and then disappear and never be seen again. This has the effect of suggesting that ethics is something exalted and unconnected with one's everyday moral concerns. The second stage takes place during clinical teaching, and the idea is that the student acquires an 'ethical' grasp from observing the practice of an experienced professional. Just as the novice surgeon or the nursing student picks up knowledge and techniques from watching an experienced practitioner so ethics is expected to be absorbed. This stage, of course, presupposes that the senior's practice is exemplary, which it may not be, and that there is no room for other ways of looking at moral questions.

The basic assumption, common to both stages of the traditional method, is that explicit or implicit instruction must always be given exclusively by a senior member of the relevant profession—thus reinforcing the idea that 'ethics' is an occult matter whose mysteries are not for the layman or the inexperienced student. Criticism by outsiders of current practices is seen as 'doctor bashing' and the idea that the professional could sometimes learn from outsiders, or from juniors in the profession, is not thinkable.

This description is no doubt exaggerated but has sufficient truth in it to warrant some suggestions for other ways of proceeding. It should like to suggest that the following factors are important for improving the teaching of morality in health care contexts, and therefore for improving health care. Attention must be given to:

1. The 'shape' of the teaching environment.
2. The content of what is taught.
3. How it is taught.
4. Who teaches it.
5. The example set in the hospital or any other care environment.

1. Whereas it is important that there should be lectures or other formal ways of teaching ethics in college or university—this is necessary to provide the conceptual framework—this teaching will come to nothing unless it is explicitly integrated with the practice experiences of the student and is seen to be relevant. The teachers at each stage must know and refer to what has already been said, and above all the practitioners must take up relevant points and illustrate them. There should be co-ordination.

2 and 3. The content and method of teaching will depend on resources but it is important to encourage *critical* discussion of a *realistic* sort. Thus, a student might be asked to discuss a care approach and then to say what *he* would have done. Whereas much of the material for such discussions will involve case histories and moral philosophy, it is important to remember that novels, poems, plays or films can make a large impact on a student and develop intuitive understanding.

4. The fourth of the factors to be noted as important in moral education concerns the matter of *who* should be involved. It is helpful if the enterprise is a co-operative one with people outside the particular profession. For the professionals to do it all themselves gives a recipe for conservatism and whitewash, but if the classes are taken entirely by others then the students may not regard them with sufficient seriousness. Co-operation is essential although not always easy to arrange. Moral philosophers, social scientists and lawyers have an important place in teaching; so do patients and relatives who contribute a quite different slant on moral problems.

5. The fifth factor in moral education is the influence of seniors. Students will learn just as much or more from what is actually done in the real situation as from what is said. The teamwork between professionals of more than one discipline can be effective as an example in learning and teaching moral values.

To sum up, the teaching of medical ethics requires the provision of conceptual frameworks, integration with practice and the use of interested teachers from non-medical disciplines.

4.6. Conclusion

In this chapter I have tried to weaken the sharp distinctions traditionally drawn between medicine thought of as a 'profession' and other occupations. As a consequence, I have argued that although medicine will have its special moral problems we do not need a special sort of morality—'medical ethics'—to deal with them. But medicine has resource problems. There is therefore the need for firmer financial guidelines for individual practitioners and more public debate on the social ethics of resource allocation. These are problems of morality as well as of expertise, and morality can, up to a point, be taught.

References

Coleridge, Samuel Taylor (1817). *Biographia Literaria* Chapter 14. Dent, London.

Downie, R. S. and Calman, K. C. (1987). *Healthy Respect* Chapter 1. Faber and Faber, London.

Gillon, Ranaan (1986). More on professional ethics. *Journal of Medical Ethics*, **12**, editorial.

Mill, J. S. (1983). *Utilitarianism* Chapter 2. (Cited from 1962 edition.) Fontana, London.

Sieghart, Paul (1985). Professions as the conscience of society. *Journal of Medical Ethics*, **11**, 117–22.

Smith, Adam (1776). *The Wealth of Nations* Book 1, Chapter III. (Cited from 1970 edition.) Penguin, Harmondsworth.

5

Economics, ethics, law, and medical conduct

PROF. DR. H. D. C. ROSCAM ABBING

Summary

This chapter discusses the influence of limits to health care on medical conduct from a legal point of view. Medical conduct is placed in the perspective of the interests of the patient on the one hand and the interests of society as a whole on the other. Special attention is paid to the use of legislation as an instrument to pursue resource allocation in health care. The relationship between legislation and professional self-regulation is also considered, together with the meaning of the professional standard as a frame within which proper medical conduct should take place. It is argued that the underlying principles in health care (i.e. respect for individual human rights and optimal implementation of the socio-economic right to health care) require an integrated approach to allocation problems.

5.1. Introduction

In the main, the discussions on limits to health care are centred around the economics of health care. Cost containment has become a central objective of governmental policies. Yet health care is not only confronted with financial limitations. However important the boundaries set by economic constraints might be, socio-economic considerations are but one set of constraints. For example medical and technological feasibility represent another limitation. Moreover health care, and medicine as part of it, find their normative frontier in the very object of health care and medicine. This constraint is of an ethical and legal nature. The application of medical procedures and techniques is justified not merely by its feasibility; there should be a relationship of fairness between the objective and the methods applied. Ethical and legal limits should be respected in medicine. Some medical procedures might for instance be unethical and also legally unacceptable because of their inhumane nature.

Medical conduct[1] is also influenced by the rights of the patient, which constitute yet another demarcation line in health care.

Clearly these broad areas of limitations to health care are of a different nature: the first is determined by and dependent on external factors ('external limits') while the others are of a more fundamental, 'internal' nature, the so-called 'internal' limits to health care (and medicine). The latter are not influenced by mere external factors or questions of external steering. Notwithstanding their different nature and their different objectives, these areas are somehow interrelated. Their ethical and legal implications represent a constraint on present day medical practice. Therefore, when considering economics and ethics in health care, we cannot confine ourselves to the external economic limits to health care and in this context to discussions about controlling the cost explosion. Moreover, the problem of containing health care costs within acceptable boundaries can not be solved by an economic approach alone. To respond adequately to current problems in health care an ethical as well as a legal approach is indispensible. It should be left to the economists to present alternative models for cost containment in health care. The discussion about their implications and an evaluation of their possible side-effects should be left to ethicists and lawyers. This will enable politicians to formulate priorities and posteriorities and to place their decisions within a social frame of acceptability and justice.

Limits to health care, whether they stem from economic constraints, from the very objective of medicine, or from the growing awareness of rights of the patient, have likewise given rise to ethical and legal considerations. They also have influenced interference by government in the health sector. Because of these limits to health care the medical profession is called upon to reconsider prevalent standards of medical practice, having regard to the economic consequences of their conduct.

The legislator is asked to ensure a just distribution of health care services, to safeguard equity and equality in health care, and to protect the patient. In doing so, the right balance has to be set between all interests involved in health care. Contradictory legal approaches in health care stemming from different objectives should be avoided so that the individual doctor–patient relationship does not suffer unduly from an economic and ethical conflict of interests.

Society's obligation to provide appropriate answers for health care needs is based, first, upon the special importance of health care, second, on differences in health status for which the individual is not accountable, and third, on the uneven distribution and unpredictability of health care needs (President's Commission 1983; Leenen 1984). In accordance with the principles of equity and equality, the distribution of available resources in health care is directed towards eliminating discrepancies in health status. Yet, in health care we have to accept some inequalities (Leenen 1984b). This does not imply, however, that selective medicine is justifiable.

A fair distribution of health care services and facilities is one of the major concerns when discussing financial limitations to health care. Principles of equity and equality clearly influence social justice in health care. However, these are not the only principles at stake when it comes to a just distribution of scarce resources. Other elements are also pertinent when considering the availability and accessibility of health care. Among these are individual human norms and values, as well as factors influencing the state of health of an individual which lie outside the scope of health care, such as inequalities stemming from differences in natural predispositions, social differences, and the like.

5.2. Human rights

When discussing economics and ethics in health care and their impact on medical conduct it is necessary to clarify first the main underlying fundamental principles. These can be found in international human rights instruments and in recommendations and guidelines stemming from international organizations. They are also reflected in professional codes of ethics and medical conduct.

Both individual and social human rights play a role in health care. Of the former the right to life, the right to physical integrity, and the right to privacy are of particular relevance. These rights are included in the 1948 Universal Declaration of Human Rights of the United Nations, the Council of Europe European Convention for the Protection of Human Rights and Fundamental Freedoms (1950) and the United Nations International Covenant on Civil and Political Rights (1966). Other international legal documents contain clauses on individual human rights. Examples of these are the Council of Europe (Parliamentary Assembly) recommendation on the rights of the sick and the dying (1976), the Council of Europe (Committee of Ministers) recommendation concerning the patient as an active participant in his own treatment (1980) and on the legal duties of doctors *vis à vis* their patients (1985). Of the codes of conduct formulated at an international level the texts adopted by the World Medical Association are particularly noteworthy. These are:

— International Code of Medical Ethics (1949–1968) and Declaration of Geneva (1948–1968).
— Declaration of Helsinki: recommendation guiding medical doctors in biomedical research involving human subjects (1964–1975–1983).
— Declaration of Sydney: statement on death (1968–1983).
— Declaration of Oslo: statement on therapeutic abortion (1970–1983).
— Declaration of Tokyo: guidelines for medical doctors concerning torture and other cruel, inhuman or degrading treatment or punishment in relation to detention and imprisonment (1975).
— Declaration of Lisbon: the rights of the patient (1981).
— Declaration of Venice: terminal illness (1983).

Individual human rights are in principle unrelated to scarcity of resources. Their foundation lies in the right of humans to self-determination, which involves human autonomy as well as human liberty. They play an important role in the individual doctor–patient relationship and represent as such a restriction on medical conduct.

Individual rights aim at protection in the individual sphere. Neither government nor society should in principle interfere with these rights. Though they are of a more or less absolute nature, at the same time they are, however, socially limited, simply because humans are part of society.

Social human rights on the other hand are by their very nature dependent on the concrete economic resources of a country. They involve rights to participate in social goods (Leenen 1966). The right to health care is among the social rights which are also laid down in international documents: the Universal Declaration of Human Rights of the United Nations (1948); the European Social Charter of the Council of Europe (1962); and the United Nations International Covenant on Economic, Social, and Cultural Rights (1966).

The right to health care may be viewed as an instruction to governments to take necessary steps so that all citizens are able to secure an adequate level of care without excessive cost (of whatever form) to the patient. The scope of this right depends on the economic, social, and cultural conditions of the community. Decisions on the implementation of the right to health care belong to the social policy of a state. Depending on available funds, such implementation will cover more or fewer medical services. As a so-called 'claim-right' it is of a promotional nature. From among the aspects of the right to health care we can distinguish the right to care of the requisite standard, the right to health services that are geographically well distributed and the right to health services that are financially accessible (and affordable).

There is a difference in nature between the individual and social human rights. This applies to both their structure and their methods of implementation. Yet they do have a relationship; both categories of human rights are interdependent. The social rights could not exist without the cognisance of individual liberty and freedom. Their realization has to take into account the existence of individual rights so as not to lead to negation of individual freedom. On the other hand the individual rights are promoted through the exercise of social rights. Overemphasizing individual rights may come into conflict with social justice. Failure to take into account individual rights in implementing social policy may lead to affronts to human dignity (Leenen *et al*. 1986). A proper balance in the simultaneous realization of these two categories of fundamental rights will ensure the optimal protection of the individual human being (Roscam Abbing 1979). It is obvious that the right to health care has to be considered in relation to a number of other social human rights, such as the right to food, to housing, and to social security as

well as the right to employment. Individual human rights are also prominent in health care. Sometimes these rights will conflict with the right to
health care. This is the case when community interests override the
individual's interests to, for instance, privacy and personal freedom.
Examples of such a situation are compulsory vaccination and quarantine.
Complementary to the right to health care is, for instance, the right to life,
which would have no meaning if the individual were not properly protected
against illness or in case of disease would not be adequately cared for.
Other examples are the prohibition of torture and the safeguarding against
medical experimentation, the latter only being permitted with the free
consent of the person concerned and with a view to appropriate health care
(advances in treatment methods).

While it is recognized that not every country views health care from the
perspective of human rights, the issues at stake do not vary. Whether or not
one develops the case for achieving equitable access to health care through
the assertion of a right to health care, or, depending on the angle of
incidence and the legal system of a country, through a moral or ethical
(societal) obligation or a moral or ethical (individual) right, appropriate
actions to secure adequate health care for all are the subject of debate in
many countries. Referral may be made in this context to the preamble of
the constitution of the World Health Organization in which it is formulated
that 'The enjoyment of the highest attainable standard of health is one of
the fundamental rights of every human being'. The target set by the WHO
'health for all in the year 2000' may be viewed in this perspective.

However, it is not put to discussion that there are three main aspects
involved with (the right to) health care, that is, governmental responsibility
for quality of care, for availability of health care services, and for their
financial accessibility. Whether health care is viewed as a societal right or
as a social obligation, there is in neither case an unlimited, unconditional
obligation to provide health care, regardless of needs and costs; on the
contrary, as was stated above, governmental obligations are limited; the
right to health care is not an open-ended issue. It finds its restrictions,
amongst other considerations, in the constraints of limited economic
resources.

5.3. Economic constraints

Notwithstanding the fact that, unlike the Netherlands, not every country
recognizes the constitutional right to health care, health care delivery is
ensured in one way or another, through regulative activities (for instance
regarding entitlements for beneficiaries of a health coverage programme or
the quantity of health care services available).

This being so, the difficult issue arises of how to distribute scarce resources justly. In other words, at the national level, governments are faced with the dilemma of how to stimulate economizing in health care while at the same time upholding basic principles such as equity, equality, social justice, and solidarity on the one hand and patient rights on the other. At the individual level doctors are confronted with the dilemma of how to contribute to this goal when arbitrating between community interests and patients' needs.

The governmental involvement in health care to safeguard these principles is likely to be intensified at a time when there is both a decrease in financial provision and an increase in medical and medico-technical possibilities. Cost increases, fuelled by the expansion of advanced as well as routine medical procedures, at a time when financial resources are restricted, inevitably leads to greater involvement and influence from the legislators.

From a study of the trends in health legislation in Europe (Leenen *et al*. 1986) it appears that measures taken by governments include the following:

— the reinforcement of primary medical care with a view to reducing expensive inpatient care;
— the decrease in the number of beds in hospitals by such means as transforming some of them into 'care beds', particularly for elderly patients;
— legislation measures to control and/or fix rates for hospital nursing;
— increases in the personal share of the beneficiaries of social security in payment of hospitalization costs;
— control of the supply of providers of health care by means, *inter alia*, of the *numerus clausus* in medical faculties and of regulation of the setting up of specialist and general practitioner practices.
— the imposition of scales of fees for the services of health care providers;
— restrictions on services made available;
— budget systems;
— restrictions on services provided free of charge.

Generally, the necessity of cutting down health care expenditure is not questioned in the light of the overall policy to reduce (or maintain) the proportion of the national budget spend on health care. In order to (re)distribute scarce resources equitably, needs have to be assessed and priorities as well as posteriorities have to be established. In doing so, the needs of various distinct categories of patients have to be weighed against each other on the basis of unbiased criteria. The setting of priorities in health care involves assessing the need for health care services and facilities in society as a whole and a legal-ethical analysis of the distribution problem, together with political decision making. So far developments in medical science and technology have had a great impact on these kinds of decisions, rather than on the real needs of a population. Naturally, professional interests are also involved. The patient, as a central figure in health care, has been gradually pushed into the background. The patient, at least in some environments, is likely to become a tool in the hands of researchers and health care providers. This trend towards the alienation and depersonalization of health care services might be strengthened by budgetary restraints. The individual doctor-patient relationship is suffering not only from this development, but also from other tendencies such as those directed towards commercialization and marketing.

Moreover, professionalization in health care is accompanied by the downgrading of the patient as an individual and of his right to self-determination. The dependence of the patient within the health care system is simultaneously increased. In a predominantly cure-orientated health care system, personal care is becoming more and more of secondary importance. There is a growing discrepancy between the basic objective of medicine—to provide treatment for every disease or pathological condition—on the one hand, and the right of the individual to refuse treatment and to have his privacy protected on the other.

It is inevitable that governmental measures regarding ways and means of securing fairness in access to health services in times of economic constraints are likely to influence medical practice either directly or indirectly. They may in particular have consequences for the quality of care delivered. As stated in a Council of Europe (Committee of Ministers) recommendation on 'medical care universally available' (1986, Recommendation no. 5) financial difficulties ought not to result in reducing the range of services available nor their quality.

Regarding the health care delivery aspect, professional autonomy, professional codes, and professional competence and ability are under discussion. The prevalent norms and standards are inadequate to meet current problems stemming from advances in medicine and health care. Evidently, not only medical progress, but also the economic impact of health care services and facilities, have changed the conditions under which medicine is practised. Previous determinants of medical conduct (including the *'primum non nocere'* principle and the 'maximum benefit of the patient' maxim) have to be adapted to present day requirements. Thus, doctors' obligations cannot be confined merely to the observing of medical professional standards. Societal issues and requirements have also to be taken into account.

For medical conduct to be acceptable to society, the doctor has to act according to professional standards. These are composed of three elements: the medical professional standards *per se*, the duties to the patient (i.e. respect of the rights of the patient), and societal obligations (including consideration of the economic consequences of medical practice). As to medical professional standards, their scope is determined by medical science and medical experience (Leenen 1985a). The duty of the physician to abstain from treatment if the patient so wishes is a legal and moral obligation in the individual doctor–patient relationship, based upon the rights of the patient. Finally, social rules which may set limits to medical practice have to be respected.

In order to avoid civil, penal, or disciplinary liability or administrative sanctions, the physician ought to comply with these three aspects of professional standards.

5.4. Economizing and professional standards

Over the years, the physician's behaviour has become increasingly influenced by external conditions. Prospective payment schemes (DRG, diagnosis-related groups), review organizations (PRO, peer review organizations; PSRO, professional standard review organizations), consensus conferences, accreditation norms, certificates of need (CON) and the like are some examples of current external constraints on medical conduct.

The same holds true for schemes in which insurer and provider are combined (HMO, Health Maintenance Organization). HMOs are part of the competition strategy which in some countries is being developed for health care. They are supposed to act as a catalyst for improving the overall performance of the health system (Johnson 1986). At the same time they can influence medical care greatly.

From the economist's viewpoint these and other instruments will contribute to optimizing the health of the population within the limits of resources available (Mooney 1984). In order to call a halt to uncontrolled growth in health care expenditure governments will strive to subject health care providers to such instruments. In fact, quantitative criteria seem to become more important than qualitative ones. Through this latter trend the medical profession is entering an era of standardization and uniformity of medical procedures. Not only will the doctor no longer find himself in a position to adapt these procedures to the needs of the individual patient. The patient will also no longer be free in his choice of alternative methods. Uniform standards of diagnostic methods and of therapeutic procedures lead to conservative medicine and to conformity. Further, they evoke defensive medicine and, through this, will ultimately lead to a decrease in the quality of care. A discussion on the values of medicine and health care involving all parties concerned is necessary to preserve human dignity in a technologically orientated and computerized health care system.

To safeguard proper medical conduct, professional standards should be flexible and leave room for adaptation to real situations. External regulations intended to stimulate—for economic reasons—the use of standards and other uniforming models in health care equally should take these requisites into account. If not, medical practice will become embedded in a rigid system, thus encasing medical care, jeopardizing medical autonomy and endangering patients' interests (Leenen 1983).

Increase in costs of health care is undoubtedly a societal issue. Rationing of medical resources is a responsibility of governments, taking into account societal needs and professional advice. It is up to society to make the decision to limit the availability of specific types of medical care. Given this availability it is then up to the physician to decide whether and/or which medical procedure should be suggested to the individual patient, in the light of their probable pay-off and their degree of possible harm, as well as the costs involved in relation to the benefits. In this context the only proper criterion is to justify the choice of the diagnostic method and therapeutic procedures on the basis of the medical problems of the individual patient, whether or not this complies with (external) uniform standards. This direct causal link between medical conduct and the specific problems of the individual patient also excludes unnecessary examinations and procedures. Unnecessary as well as pointless medical acts are not in conformity with medical professional standards, are in conflict with patients' rights, and place undue financial burdens upon society. Patients should be protected against senseless or harmful care. Societal obligations require the application of the least costly treatment and diagnostic procedures. DRGs, for instance, when linked with prospective payment schemes, may well contain incentives for the doctor to choose diagnostic and therapeutic overkill: the most profitable DRG will be chosen, in order not to put the provider at economic risk. The patient's benefit may then become secondary to personal profit.

Regulations and other forms of third-party control, based primarily on economic considerations, can on the other hand never be used as a medical justification for not acting in accordance with patients' needs. If through the influence of law, medical conduct becomes inspired by mainly financial constraints and not so much by the particular medical context of the particular case, the physician will not then be acting according to ethical and legal principles and may be held liable for bad medical practice. Deviation from the medical professional standard is legally unacceptable. This standard is the baseline of medical professional autonomy. In other words, the medical act has to be in concurrence with the state of the art, has to be indicated by the concrete medical problems of the patient, ought not to be medically pointless, and has to be proportional to the goal which is sought. When acting in accordance with these principles, economic constraints will not come into conflict with professional duty. It goes without saying that the medical procedures, to be professionally acceptable and to be kept updated, ought to be subjected to auditing and other assessment procedures which are designed to protect and improve the quality of work undertaken by health care providers.

Professional standards also represent the frame of reference for the physician when facing the dilemma of how much more to do for the patient and determining when benefits become very small or even represent iatrogenic risks. Professional excellence and high-quality care may indeed sometimes suggest a decision *not* to spend, this in itself not being evidence of bad medical practice. Moreover, the patient has an important role when it comes to deciding about medical procedures. The physician should respect the patient's autonomy and the patient's rights. To stimulate rational economic conduct he should not only inform the patient about risks and benefits and possible alternatives, but also promote cost consciousness on the part of the consumer.

When practising medicine, the doctor will be inclined to put at the disposal of his patient every feasible medical procedure. General priority setting, with a view to obtaining an equitable distribution of resources, presupposes on the other hand co-operation from the medical profession. Thus, for instance, a reserved attitude is required from the medical profession in the context of the first application of advanced programmes. The policy decision on their availability ought to precede their introduction. Sometimes it is argued that such a reserved attitude is contradictory to proper medical conduct. However, proper medical conduct is not synonymous with doing everything technically feasible for each patient. The introduction of new programmes and techniques is a societal decision and cannot be left to the medical profession alone. The social dimension of professional standards is in fact contradictory to such a unilateral approach. The social function of medicine does not allow for leaving decisions on the introduction of new, often highly sophisticated and costly, diagnostic and therapeutic techniques to the medical profession alone. Before introducing a new health care service or facility, a decision ought to be made on whether the new procedure is of substantial value and, if so, whether the resources required for it will be available, or whether preference is to be given to other sectors of health care. If the medical profession does not comply with these conditions, the legislator will have to intervene to avoid, *inter alia*, inequities in health services.

5.5. Ethical and legal considerations

Not only is financial priority setting at stake; ethical and legal considerations are also involved. In fact not everything that is technically feasible is automatically ethically justified. Also the rights of the patient have to be considered. Naturally, it should be left to the individual patient to establish his own limits when it comes to undergoing medical interventions. Moreover, to do 'more' in medicine does not necessarily imply that the extra results in an improved level of health. To put marginally effective, but expensive, treatment at the disposal of a small group of patients might be contrary to equity in health care. In this respect quality of life may play a role when it comes to deciding at the governmental level on availability of new medical treatment facilities. On the other hand, the quality of life may not play a role in decisions by physicians. The judgement on the individual quality of life can only be made by the patient (Leenen 1985a). Society is called upon to delineate the acceptability of medical interventions, having regard to both their nature and their possible side-effects and misuse. It is a matter for society to discuss whether the possible achievements of medical research are ethically and legally acceptable. Only when humanitarian values are not at stake, there is professional consensus on medical effectiveness, it is socially acceptable, and the benefits outweigh the costs can political decisions about a new technique follow within the framework of economic considerations. Cost–benefit analyses are a useful tool to facilitate such decision making, provided they are not applied only to the new method. Also relevant are other considerations, such as alternatives available, the degree of urgency, the number of persons likely to benefit, and so on. If not carefully used and structured, cost–benefit analyses will be too compartmentalized and fragmentary. They might then well result in a discriminatory approach to special categories of patients.

Moreover, if a new method is introduced but—for economic reasons—its availability is limited, we are faced with the difficult issue of selection of patients. This might constitute a conflict of interests which has to be resolved by the physician in the individual doctor–patient relationship. As was indicated above, cost-saving and cost–benefit analysis may never be treated by a doctor as a legitimate ethical basis for witholding life-saving or life-supporting treatment (Stone 1985). Therefore, when available services are thus limited, society must be called upon to discuss and accept selection criteria. Differences in health status, age, social class, ability to pay, and social behaviour ought not to play a role when selecting patients. When the selection issue arises, medical conditions should dominate. It should be left to the medical profession to establish criteria for medical necessity in accordance with medical professional standards. It should be left to society to fix procedural conditions to be considered in a selection system and to establish—whenever necessary—objective selection criteria other than strictly medical ones (Leenen 1985b). In whatever way a selection system is formulated, principles of fairness and equity have to be respected. The patient selection issue, moreover, gives rise to some general ethical imperatives. Thus, the physician is not only under an ethical but also under a legal obligation to be efficient and to avoid waste. Effective and efficient administration, management, and decision-making procedures, as well as avoidance of bureaucracy, will influence the scarcity problem favourably. Also the individual patient should avoid unnecessary consumption.

5.6. Legislative measures

Legislative and other regulatory measures likewise should be efficient and effective. Compensation for failures in the health care system through complicated and burdensome regulative measures is counter-productive. Ineffective regulation does not become effective through additional legislation. The role of the legislator in health care undoubtedly has expanded during the last decades. The reasons for this are manifold. First, there is a growing awareness that health care is a public utility. Therefore it is logical that the law is applied as an instrument to steer the health care system. Economic considerations also underly the increase in legislative and regulative measures. But public responsibility and cost-containment considerations require regulation of the health care system, of the quality of care delivered, of the quantity of services and facilities available, and of the use of services.

Legislation will also help to keep a reasonable balance regarding the powers of different 'actors' in the system as well as protecting disadvantaged groups. Promotion of health and protection of the health of the population at large may be other motives for legislation. To protect the individual patient, regulative measures may also be needed. The law is instrumental in striking the proper balance between the public interest and the needs of the individual.

The negative aspects of legislation should, however, not be overlooked. This holds in particular when governments consider using legislation as an instrument for the implementation of economic policies. Some of these negative aspects are that legislation never covers all aspects of a subject, that it may lead to rigidity, and that it often stimulates bureaucracy. There is a risk of overregulation. Moreover, the existence of legislation does not automatically imply its observance. Also, legislation may invoke effects which were not contemplated.

As indicated previously, governments are inclined to subject the decision processes in medical practice to legislation or other forms of regulation. It was further pointed out that this might be contrary to the nuances of individual medical problems. Undue interference by the legislator in medical conduct will not be in the interest of the patient. Therefore careful use should be made of the law when used as an instrument to implement cost-containment methods.

Moreover, legislation is but one of the appropriate instruments for controlling the use of health care services and facilities. Other valuable methods are informing the public about healthy conduct, promoting cost consciousness on the part of consumers and suppliers of health care, and encouraging preventive measures. Only through serious discussion of the real objectives involved and investigations into alternatives for legislation can effective and efficient legislative policy be developed (Leenen 1985b).

Legislation or other regulative measures directed towards quality control have become increasingly important in health care. Indeed, the regulation of health professions is one of the oldest subjects to be dealt with by the legislator. Access to the professions, their functioning and their structure are the main aspects covered by legislation in many countries (Leenen *et al.* 1986). Over the last few years, existing legislation on training has been revised because of the many changes which have taken place in medical practice. Thus, the influence of the development of medical sciences and medical techniques has been unmistakable. There is a growing tendency to reform legislation in such a way that it comprises a description of functions of doctors and other health care providers. Moreover, legislation on training has been influenced by various international organizations (WHO, Council of Europe, European Communities).

Traditionally, the medical profession was autonomous in its decisions and choices regarding existing or new medical procedures, irrespective of the costs involved. The emancipation of the patient, which finds expression in the formulation of the rights of the patient, is one of the elements which has restricted this autonomy. These rights are a prominent issue in health care. The duties of the health care providers, as laid down in professional codes or even in law, are derived from these rights and not vice versa!

Another reason for the restriction of medical autonomy may be found in the necessity for priority setting as well as posteriority setting (de Lange 1984). The present situation also calls for reflection upon the beneficiaries of, and coverage by, social insurance schemes. Until recently, such schemes initiated almost unlimited claims. Notions such as 'customary in the profession' and 'whenever a medical indication is prevalent' were the only criteria available to help to check whether a claim was justified or not. In an attempt to control such an almost uncontrollable system, not only were financial contributions by patients introduced, but there has also been a tendency towards trying to regulate medical indications in relation to specific conditions. But trends are likely to influence medical conduct.

In general, when considering intervention through law much will depend on the question of whether and to what extent professional self-regulation functions. The more the medical profession is successful in limiting its production, and in delivering quality care, the less the legislator will be inclined to intervene. Unfortunately, so far the medical profession itself has not mastered the situation. Consequently the legislator has been forced to interfere in medical decision making. Legislation is then used to provide a countervailing power against the monopolistic position of the medical profession.

The necessity for legal measures affecting medical conduct is not disputed. Because of the failure of the medical profession to control not only the quantity but also the quality of care delivered, this responsibility has to be carried out by public authorities. Of course this does not necessarily imply that professional autonomy will be violated. In so far as such autonomy is bounded by medical professional standards, the legislator may not interfere with it. External regulations cannot limit these standards, and therefore, as indicated above, ought not to constitute a justification in the hands of physicians to withold or stop medically necessary treatment. The legislator can formulate standards for care, can set rules for the decision making of physicians, impose quality assessment, and so forth, but the legislator cannot intervene in the medical act itself.

The existence of a need for regulative measures does not in itself mean that the affected groups are in no way involved. A dialogue between the legislator and those who are the object of legislation is indicated in order to make regulation socially acceptable. Moreover, there is a need for a cautious attitude on the part of the legislator when considering the regulation of medical conduct. Some aspects of this have already been indicated. Among other reasons should be mentioned the complexity and multi-faceted nature of medical conduct, which makes it difficult to encompass in legislation, the impossibility of guaranteeing, through law, a particular standard of individual medical conduct, and so on.

These and other considerations are also relevant when considering the method of legislation to be used. For many reasons, the so-called 'indirect' legislation seems preferable to direct interference (Leenen 1985a). This method involves the government's setting a structural and procedural framework within which medical conduct should then take place. Within this framework the responsibility for specific medical conduct is left to the physician. For instance legislation may prescribe medical audit, the keeping of patients' files, and the functioning of complaint procedures, and formulate criteria with a view to developing standards for medical conduct.

In such a method, the legislator abstains from interfering with specific medical conduct directly, but creates the conditions within which medical conduct should take place, so that steering and control are possible. It is then left to the medical profession to elaborate on these legal conditions through self-regulation. Public and professional responsibility are thus kept in harmony (Roscam Abbing 1984). In this context, quality control is one of the main features of professional self-regulation. Yet it appears from a WHO study that practically no country has taken legal or regulatory measures in this respect (Leenen *et al*, 1986). Quality control is regulated by general and normal rules (supervision by the ministry of public health as well as by the professional organization). Professional codes of ethics and standards of professional conduct also play a role with a view to regulating medical conduct in health care. The law may stimulate the drawing up (and revision) of such codes and standards, so that they are placed in the context of general health policy, the rights of the patients, and the tasks of other health workers. Generally, however, legislators in Europe do not interfere in special medical procedures, leaving it to the profession to see that they are carried out expertly.

While, in general, professional attitudes in health care are determined by professional codes governing ethics and conduct, they are, according to some specialists, too general in nature to give concrete guidance to health care professionals. A criticism of such professional codes may be that they are too idealistic and sometimes even internally contradictory. It has also been suggested that they are used to legitimate the activities of a professional group rather than to provide a framework for proper care. These somewhat negative views on the purpose and scope of professional codes in health care are, however, countered by the views of most experts, who tend to favour them. It should not be overlooked that they undoubtedly have their value. They help to demarcate what is considered to be acceptable conduct in health care. Thus, they may provide a guarantee that improper medical interventions are avoided and thereby provide a basis for disciplinary proceedings before both the courts and professional tribunals or other disciplinary bodies. To function properly such codes should, however, comply with certain conditions. They should in particular have the support of the professional group concerned and be open to discussion by the public at large. Moreover, they should not merely protect the interests of the profession concerned, but should also service the public interest. Finally, they need to be continually reviewed both nationally and internationally, in order to adapt them to new developments. Professional codes of ethics and conduct should be orientated towards standards acceptable to society as a whole, and at the same time leave sufficient room for individual ethical viewpoints. The legislator ought to help to stimulate this process. Basic legal and social norms should, however, be laid down in law. In order to remain humane, to respect individual freedom and dignity in health care, and, at the same time, to guarantee equal access to health care for all, current moral, ethical, and legal dilemmas require open discussion on a continuing basis. It is only through continuous reflection on the threats to human dignity, equality, and social justice stemming from a blind application of all available medico-technical possibilities on the one hand and inconsiderate and biased economic measures on the other, that we can guarantee respect for fundamental human rights, such as the right to life, the right to bodily and physical integrity, and the right to privacy, as well as the right to health care. It is the task of the legislator to promote social justice and an equitable distribution of the available health services as well as to protect human values and norms.

The allocation problems have to be solved within the context of the socio-economic right to health care. The protection of individual human rights and liberties, however, ought also to be taken into account when developing cost-containment policies. If not, the professional autonomy in the doctor–patient relation will be unduly restricted and professional standards will be jeopardized. While recognizing the need for the just allocation of scarce health resources, there needs to be a careful balancing of the weight to be attached to cost-containment policies against that to be attached to the interests of the individual patient.

Notes

1. This paper is restricted to considerations of the conduct of the medical profession. Most arguments are however also relevant to other professions in health care.

References

Johnson, A. N. (1986). The impact of health maintenance organizations and competition on hospitals in Minneapolis, St. Paul. *Journal of Health Politics, Policy and Law*, **10**(4), Winter 659–764.

Lange de, S. A. (1984). *Over grenzen van de curatieve gezondheidszorg*.

Leenen, H. J. J. (1966). *Sociale grondrechten en gezondheidszorg*. Alphen a/d Rijn, De Boer/Brandt, Hilversum.

Leenen, H. J. J. (1983). Standaard van zorg en vrijheid van keuze. In E. v.d. Weg, (ed.) *Standaard van zorg en keuzevrijheid*. Maatschappij en Gezondheid, 4, Tijdstroom, Lochem.

Leenen, H. J. J. (1984a). Gelijkheid en ongelijkheid in de gezondheidszorg. *T. v. Gezondheidsrecht*, **2**, 53–68.

Leenen, H. J. J. (1984b) Prioriteiten stellen in de gezondheidszorg. *Medisch Contact*, **41**, 1323–4.

Leenen, H. J. J. (1985a). Legal aspects of clinical autonomy. *Health Policy*, **5**, 3–14.

Leenen, H. J. J. (1985b). Regulation and selection of patients. *Health Policy* **4**, 265–72.

Leenen H. J. J., G. Pinet and A. V. Prims (1986). *Trends in health legislation in Europe*. WHO, Copenhagen, Masson (France).

Mooney, G. (1984). Medical ethics an excuse for inefficiency. *Journal of Medical Ethics*, **10**, 183–5.

President's Commission for the study of ethical problems in medicine and bio-medical and behaviorial research (1983). *Securing access to health care.* Vol. I, March. Washington, D.C.: US Government Printing Office.

Roscam Abbing, H. D. C. (1979). *International organizations in Europe and the right to health care.* Kluwer, Deventer.

Roscam Abbing, H. D. C. (1984). De Heelmeester op het rechte(n) spoor. *Medisch Contact*, **45**, 1455–7.

Stone (1985). Law's influence on medicine and medical ethics. *New England Journal of Medicine*, **312**(5), 309–12.

6

Financing of medical services and medical ethics

PATRICIA SOHL

Summary

This chapter examines the relationship between economics and medical ethics in a historical setting. Going back as far as the fifth century BC, it shows that at various times since and in various different ways the economic framework for the delivery of medical services has had some influence on the nature of medical ethics.

The chapter quotes the Declaration of Copenhagen on Health Care Costs, showing how this clearly delimits direct physician responsibility to patient care. Finally against the larger historical background the chapter speculates about the present day relationship between health care financing and medical ethics.

6.1. Introduction

The doctors of the European Economic Community . . . believe it is their duty to collaborate in researching measures which aim at a better use and rationalisation of measures set aside for health care, on the express condition that in all circumstances, the freedom of prescription of the doctor, the natural defender of every patient, should be respected.

This is a part (the full statement is attached as an appendix to this chapter) of the Declaration of Copenhagen on Health Care Costs issued by the Standing Committee of Physicians to the Common Market in 1979. There is a sense in which it sums up current dilemmas about medical ethics and economics in health care. What is clear, however, is that the dilemmas are not new. This chapter attempts to place these dilemmas in a historical perspective.

Medical practitioners in their daily work concern themselves with concrete cases of threats to the health of identifiable individuals; health economists in their daily work concern themselves with the aggregate effects of such persons, that is they work at the level of social planning. The provision of medical services is an individualized and personal process valued by society, which grants much autonomy and privacy to the participants. Medical oaths and codes have spoken to the moral aspects of this interhuman relationship since the time of Hippocrates. These ethical statements serve as guidelines to the individual physician reminding them of the standards set by the collective moral wisdom, if you will, of other physicians. They can be seen to function as a guarantee given by the profession to society: these standards we promise you. What is interesting about the codes and declarations is that they seem to be generated in times of competition threatening the market position of the physicians. As such, economic conditions have been relevant in their formation. The question for this conference was to what extent economics had influenced ethics. And since Hippocratic duties are often claimed in current debates about efficiency and responsibility for the excessive costs of medical services, let us look at the evolution of concepts considered essential to the practice of medicine throughout history.

6.2. The emergence of the medical practitioner from an itinerant craftsman in the fifth century BC to a virtuous professional in the second century AD

Physicians had been itinerant craftsmen from Homeric times. Even in the classical age few stayed in their home city or established a permanent residence. Thus, they were not integrated into a community and avoided the common social pressures that tend to insure the reliability of craftsmen. There were no medical schools, and no civil authorities regulated the practice of medicine until after Roman times (Edelstein 1967a). To the extent that a person was interested in acquiring medical skills the training roughly approximated to apprenticing oneself to a master.

In terms of economic structure, the classical period had no concept of profession. Work was a dire necessity, not 'ennobling', and artists and physicians were judged on a par with other manual workers. The standard was one of expertness of performance. One was a good *x* if one did the work of *x*s well. Regarding physicians who practised medicine, Hippocrates speaks of the appropriate subject for their craft in *The arts*. As the reader will recall, the collection of writings called the Hippocratic Corpus was authored over three centuries. *The arts* is one of the oldest works dated in the fifth century BC.

... I will define what I conceive medicine to be. In general terms, it is to do away with the sufferings of the sick, to lessen the violence of their diseases, and to refuse to treat those who are over-ministered by their diseases, realizing that in such cases medicine is powerless (Hippocrates, *The arts*).

The term used by the true physicians in setting themselves apart from the charlatan (i.e. the competition) is that of 'expertness' which is at the same time 'goodness'. In Plato's *Republic* the fact that the physician charges fees for medical services, or in other words was on a remuneration system based on 'fee-per-item of service' is acceptable to Socrates so long as the aim of the art takes precedence over the fee earning: 'Unless pay is added to it there would be no benefit to the craftsman, and consequently he would be unwilling to go to the trouble of taking care of the troubles of others' (Plato,) *Republic*, Book 1. Aristotle agreed with this, stating in *Politics* that the function of medicine is that of producing health not wealth. He conceded that the acquisition of fees paid to the physician was necessary for there to be medical practice, but that the acquisition was not the *end* of the practice—not its reason for existing and not the criterion for evaluating its excellence or failure. As a craft, medicine was categorized under the 'arts of acquisition', which dealt with labour for hire in exchange for money.

Until the third century BC there were no moral demands for virtue required of craftsmen by society beyond doing one's task well. In *Nichomachean ethics*, Aristotle writes that moral virtue isn't necessary for producing a good product. The moral goodness of craftsmen was their own affair.

However, the Pythagoreans were 'ahead of their time' in believing even in the fifth century BC that the work of craftsmen had moral components and that artists *could* achieve 'the good' by doing their work well. The Hippocratic tradition of medicine is the tradition of the Pythagoreans, its practices and values encoded in the Corpus dealing with both the ethical and scientific aspects. In the 'Oath' a personal ethics is prescribed for the physician, infusing a strong moral commitment into the practice of medicine (Edelstein 1967b).

Later, in Hellenistic times, the Stoics believed that the moral order *was* compatible with the acquisition of money through any kind of work, and they taught that all persons including artisans (and hence, physicians) can and must live up to the rules of ethics. This means that the ethics of good craftsmanship could be expanded and indeed the moral issues latent in the Pythagorean teachings became evident in the works in the Hippocratic Corpus written between 300 and 100 BC *On the physician* and *Precepts*. It is here we find that the details of how to deal with the economic issues of being an itinerant physician are subsumed under the moral idea of being a good healer. From *Precepts*:

IV. So one must not be anxious about fixing a fee. For I consider such a worry to be harmful to a troubled patient, particularly if the disease be acute . . . Therefore, it is better to reproach a patient you have saved than to extort money from those who are at death's door (Hippocrates, *Precepts*)

This is practical advice for someone who must live by reputation as an itinerant service provider. (It is clearly also one of the arguments for insurance today.) But also, in addition to these 'business' concerns the advice given addresses the moral content of the nature and function of the art.

Writings in the third century BC give evidence of the changes which followed the decline of both ancient religion and the city state as guiding factors for moral behaviour. The successors of Aristotle distinguished 'the happy life' and 'the good life'—the one presupposing independent means, the other to be led by someone who had an occupation. In both, moral law is to be fulfilled. Virtue or morality then became increasingly identified not with the objective content of human actions but rather with the inner attitude of the performer. The principal criterion of right or wrong came to be found almost exclusively in the proper use of things, good or bad, rather than in the things themselves. The crafts were then seen in a new (Pythagorean) light.

For our purposes it is interesting that at the turn of the fourth to the third century BC in the Pseudegraphic Platonic dialogue *Eryxias* (the only extant Greek treatise that deals exclusively with economic problems) there is disagreement with Aristotle's idea of the crafts as 'limited servitude' for monetary exchange. Instead, in the discussion between wealth and virtue the crafts are to be classified under 'possession of wealth' and are thus 'more noble'. The 'skilled physician' is an example given in the conversation. This legitimized what Pythagorean medical ethics had held for two centuries.

The Hippocratic work *On decorum* was written slightly after *Eryxias*. In it we find self-control, regularity of habits, justness and fairness, and a proper and good behaviour prescribed for the 'soul' of the physician—the 'mean between extremes' of an Aristotelean gentleman. *On decorum* deals with general moral considerations in medical practice, but does so with a new respect for the 'wisdom' of the physician. Not only was the nature of the world view of medicine as a craft changing; the type of knowledge on which the art was based was also evolving. From Pythagorean practice of observation, medicine became more scientific and philosophical. The moral concerns implicit in fifth-century BC Pythagorean empiricism were becoming explicit. The physician's stance, newly improved by being able to achieve both virtue and wisdom, slowly changed from viewing the patient as an object of the medical art and skill, to being a fellow human to whom the physician is *duty* bound, due to the very nature of his medical knowledge. Here we have what Mooney and McGuire (Chapter 2) would presumably describe in their economic language as a change in the 'commodity' health care. That is, in addition to treating the patient's illness in a competent technical manner the physician must give the patient the benefit of moral virtue. There is a repetition of the recognition that medicine is to serve all people, free or slave (and this recognition is unusual for classical times), but, in the spirit of the changes mentioned above, this requirement to serve all occurs in a new awareness of the interdependence of physician and patient. From *Precepts*:

VI. I urge you not to be too unkind, but to consider carefully your patient's superabundance or means. Sometimes give your services for nothing, calling to mind a previous benefaction or present satisfaction (your present reputation). And if there be an opportunity of serving one who is a stranger in financial straits, give assistance to all such. For where there is love of man, there is also love of the art. For some patients, though conscious that their condition is perilous, recover their health simply through their contentment with the goodness of the physician. And it is well to superintend the sick to make them well, to care for the healthy to keep them well, but also to care for one's own self, so as to observe what is seemly (Hippocrates, *Precepts*).

The unity between the ethics of an outward performance of a craft and the ethics of an inner intention become most visible at the time of the Stoic philosopher and physician, Scribonius. In the first century AD he calls medicine not merely an art or science but a profession—'the true physician is bound in lawful obedience to medicine by his oath' (Scribonius, *On remedies*). To be a physician one must not only have knowledge but must pledge (profess) to use it properly. The right standard of conduct for the role or office voluntarily undertaken by the physician is enforced upon him by the nature of medical work itself, as is the standard of adequate knowledge. Unless he knows all he ought to know and makes use of it for the benefit of the sick he fails in his duty. Scribonius admits that he is extending the 'love of humanity' beyond the 'philanthropy' of Hippocrates. The dovetailing of this humanism in first century AD Rome and that of Galen 100 years later with Christianity's principle of brotherly love, because all are equal before the eyes of God, came to be considered in medical ethics as beneficence.

The Roman talent for organization and law making established a precedent of two classes of physicians, one privileged by being in the employ of a patron (often a city), the other charging a fee for service. This precedent was to remain and indirectly cause concern until physicians formally established national medical associations in the nineteenth century. By the time of the rise of the Roman Empire physicians had become citizens and even some free-born Romans practised medicine. There was still no civil authority which regulated these basically itinerant healers. What law there was dealt only with cases of apparent death from treatment and minor issues of fee and contract agreement (Edelstein 1967).

At one point the term 'professio' meant something other than just voluntarily promising. It indicated persons required to pay taxes. But when Panaetus began the first systematic philosophical analysis of virtues particular to a profession he didn't study their incomes. His work was freely translated by Cicero in his book *On duties* in the first century BC. The argument is that of late Stoics; virtue is basically knowledge for the use of others. Cicero and Panaetus consider political and public activities the only proper ones for a gentleman, and give much attention to the duties one has to the state. For example, the judge is not permitted to be biased by friendship; in his role as judge he is not to act as friend.

The emergence in the middle of the first century AD of 'De officiis judicis' is a paradigm for all professional duty. The morality of the obligations is derived from the nature of the work and its value to the consumer (Norden 1905). The value of medicine to the state is a dimension beyond the individual morality of the patient–physician relationship. It is discussed by Quintilian in great detail, but there is little evidence of the notion being adopted into medical ethical writings. What is said is always that individual patient considerations outweigh any other.

After a period when all physicians were granted exemption from taxes and from having soldiers billeted in their houses, a *numerus clausus* was introduced limiting the number of privileged physicians in each city. Galen, who wrote on medical ethics in his essay 'The best physician is also a philosopher', rued the effect of patronage which offered security, income, and prestige to only some physicians. He urged physicians to be contemptuous of money, and rather to concentrate on their work, be self-controlled and just. We see here yet again the concern that medicine might somehow be polluted by economic incentives. Galen's extensive writings on Hippocrates and Plato often admonish the reader that it is important to distinguish between individual motives which may not be intrinsic to the pursuit of medicine.

Even the idealist Scribonius was not naive about a moral programme which rested on the love of humanity and lacked external enforcement. He argued that patients also had a responsibility for the quality of their interaction with physicians: 'Rarely does anyone make an evaluation of the doctor before putting himself and his family under his care. And yet, if people have their portrait painted, they will try to make sure of the artist's qualities on the basis which experience can tell, and then select and hire him' (Scribonius, *On Remedies*). It is a dilemma that remains today. (See Weisbrod, quoted in Mooney and McGuire, Chapter 2).

Why the Romans never enacted laws to regulate physicians is difficult to ascertain. How they dealt with the tension in medicine between idealism and the problems caused by non-idealist practitioners is illustrated by the poem of Sarapion. It literally carved into stone, above the door to the Athenian temple of Asclepius, the late Stoic belief of self-regulation. All physicians who enter are admonished:

First to heal his mind and to give assistance to himself before giving it to anyone (else), and to cure with moral courage and with proper attitude. Then he would be like god saviour and, equally of slaves, of paupers, of rich men, of princes, and to all a brother, such help he would give. For we are all brothers. Therefore he would not hate anyone, nor would he harbour envy in his mind (Maas and Oliver 1939).

This poem foreshadows the next 1500 years of Christian medical ethics. It also stands testimony to the fact that the next practical step which attempted to address the problems of the economic realities of a patronage system for physicians was the publication of Thomas Percival's *Medical ethics* in 1803. (This work, the emergence of medicine as a formally organized profession, and the ethical and economic issues surrounding this, will be discussed in the next section.)

In summary, we have seen how skilled healers, the Hippocratic craftsmen, evolved over the span of 600 or 700 years into professional physicians who could achieve not only virtue but wealth in caring for their patients. They voluntarily commited themselves to a lifestyle and an ethical behaviour as part of their activities not only because this was (1) good for 'business', but also because their business was (2) good for fellow human beings, and (3) their special knowledge served the need of ill equals. There was no civil supervision of their practices, the ethical self-regulation being acceptable to the times and later Christian-based medical ethics. The patronage possibilities for only some physicians split practitioners for the first time into two groups, neither of which could resolve the moral/practical dilemma of ethics and economics.

6.3. The emergence of medicine as a modern profession

Medical historians regard Thomas Percival's work *Medical ethics: or a code of institutes and precepts adopted to the professional conduct of physicians and surgeons* as 'the transition from the broad principles of Greek medical ethics to the current complicated system' (Leake 1927).

After an epidemic of typhus in 1789, Percival was invited by the Manchester Infirmary to draw up 'a scheme of professional conduct relative to hospitals and other medical charities'. Changes were made among the hospital staff in order to cope with the epidemic. These changes exacerbated the already existent tensions, many of which stemmed from what were in essence economic concerns and competitions between the professions, among the three groups of staff: physicians, surgeons, and apothecaries. In order to help produce a reconciliation he wrote *Medical ethics*. The four parts of the treatise provide detailed procedures for avoiding the decline of public confidence in the profession arising from open quarrelling and/or the disruption of services. The titles of his four sections show the multiplicity of the profession's moral relations which had developed. They are 'Of professional conduct, relative to hospitals, or other medical charities', 'Of the conduct of physicians towards apothecaries', 'Of professional duties in certain cases which require a knowledge of law', and 'Of professional conduct in private or general practice' (Percival 1803).

The titles of these four sections reflect more than the areas of ethical concern. They mirror the fragmented organization of medical practitioners in 1800. The most prestigious group were the physicians. Their licence to practise was granted by the Royal College of Physicians founded in 1518 (Waddington 1984a). The college required an academic education, though no medical curriculum was established until the mid nineteenth century; students read and were examined in classical languages and literature. These Christian gentlemen physicians were most often affiliated with a patron and could serve as consultants to the charitable hospitals. Percival was a well-respected member of his college, having trained at the Universities of Edinburgh and Leiden. He was a co-founder of the Society for Philosophy and Literature in Manchester and on the staff of the infirmary—a man of his time with belief in Enlightenment values of human reason.

Surgeons were not academically trained. They acquired their skills during an apprenticeship reflecting their craft guild origins. Until 1745 they were united with barbers, and in 1800 were granted their own charter—the Royal College of Surgeons of London.

General practitioners had no charter, and most earned their living only by combining private practice with farming or apothecary trade.

The apothecaries represented the last and lowest in status of medical practitioners. They were members of the Worshipful Society of Apothecaries.

That there could be serious disagreements and competition among the staff at Manchester had never occurred to anyone before. Percival concerned himself with the 'business' aspects of the various practitioner groups, interestingly seeing no conflict between these and the ethical aspects of patient care considerations. The moral basis he provided was a mix of gentlemanly virtue and Christian brotherhood. In the first edition of his work he included the sermon that his minister–physician son had delivered to the infirmary staff, wherein it was stated that the staff was dependent on the lower classes for supplies of food, clothing, shelter, and the comforts of life. It was recognized that their ability to work was related to their health and occupational conditions. It was therefore a duty for the staff to care for them as patients (Rossel 1979). There were three motives for working in the infirmary: the reputation acquired from such noble service, the interest in acquiring knowledge and experience, and the spirit of humanism. None of the patients paid, so no economic motives were discussed but the practice was that patrons were found among the board members or by referrals to their friends.

Though Percival was content with the status of medical organization, the often underemployed non-college practitioners were not. Medical sociologists have documented the difficulties if not impossibilities of non-physicians earning their living by medicine in France (Herzlich 1982), the Netherlands (Waddington 1984b), England, and the USA. There had been a growing belief that the reason for this was not that the larger public could not afford to pay for medical services but that the profession was over-crowded. William Cullen, president of the Royal College of Physicians in Edinburgh, requested Adam Smith's opinion in 1774 about the practice of some Scottish universities which sold medical diplomas sometimes without even requiring residence. Smith's reply was critical:

the facility of obtaining degrees, particularly in physic, from those poor universities, had two effects, both extremely advantageous to the public, but extremely dis-agreeable to the graduates of other universities, whose degrees had cost them much time and expense. First, it multiplied very much the number of doctors, and thereby no doubt sunk their fees, or at least hindered them from rising so very high as they otherwise would have done. Had the universities of Oxford and Cambridge been able to maintain themselves in the exclusive privilege of graduating all the doctors who could practise in England, the price of feeling a pulse might by this time have risen from two or three guineas, the price which it has now happily arrived at, to double or treble that sum . . . Secondly, it reduced a good deal the rank and dignity of a doctor (Waddington 1984c).

Restricted entry was first to emerge after the formation of national medical associations in the mid nineteenth century (British Medical Association in 1832, the Danish in 1857, the American in 1847). The arguments for restriction were abundant, from noting an ethical duty to protect the public from unqualified practitioners to purely economic arguments about protecting the income of qualified physicians. The pat-ronage system with its client control of the service provider worked against the emergence of medicine as a formally organized profession, but, with the arrival of national medical associations, doctors had access to a larger market of patients. This growth in demand for services offered medicine as a secure career and physician incomes did increase.

What developed in the nineteenth century was a growth in the demand for services, probably due to a real increase in the standard of living as well as the introduction of sliding-scale fees and the belief among the Victorian middle class that individual achievement in work necessitated paying attention to one's health (Holloway 1964). There was general optimism about progress and control of the world, including disease. Hospitals became not only the focus for a unified medical curriculum and the setting for the socialization of physicians to the scientific and ethical values of the profession, but also an institutionalized setting for central control with the profession itself. The Royal College maintained its influence, members often becoming consultants to hospitals. The association of medicine and science gave prestige and authority to physicians and decreased the need for the social connections of the patronage system, though, according to Starr (1977), 'the increased demand for medical services seems to have preceded significant improvements in the effectiveness of physicians'.

The shift to the hospital in the nineteenth century had other implications for the practice of medicine. It was within the hospital, set up to treat large numbers of low-status patients in a scientific manner, that the shift from the 'person-orientated' form of medical practice necessary to the patronage system and itinerant practice to the 'object-orientated' form of medical practice occurred (Jewson 1976). The newly formed medical associations all dealt with this new form of practice but seemed unaware of any need to stress the traditional patient-care ethical principles. Most of the codes of ethics which developed shortly after the establishment of the national medical associations looked remarkably like Percival's *Medical ethics*.

There were, however, formal bodies evolving within the profession to police its members for adherence to the standards established in the ethical codes. These General Medical Councils were the first regulatory bodies to supervise practitioners. At the same time (mid nineteenth century) the first registration boards for qualified physicians were also formed.

Although it was in the last century that social medicine began, the ethical codes of organized medicine did not speak to the issues of general or universal access to services, large-scale prevention programmes, or other utilitarian concerns. The newly emerged profession was concerned with solidifying its position on the basis of the ethical traditions of the *laissez-faire* practice of its itinerant practitioner origins. The humanism of ancient Greek medicine required no social responsibilities on the part of the physician (Galdston 1940). Even the brotherly love of nineteenth century reformers addressed only the individual patient and individual doctor (Temkin 1949).

A follower of Bentham, Edwin Chadwick, wrote in 1842 what is probably the best-known utilitarian argument for public health measures in the 'Report on the sanitary conditions of the labouring population'.

It is an appalling fact that of all who are born of the labouring classes in Manchester, more than 57% die before they attain five years of age, that is, before they can be engaged in factory labour (Campbell 1984).

In 1838 in the fourth annual report of the Poor Law Commission another argument for the usefulness of public health legislation was given by Chadwick.

All epidemics and all infectious diseases are attended with charges, immediate and ultimate on the poor rates . . . The amount of burdens thus produced is frequently so great as to render it good economy on the part of the administrators of the Poor Law to incur the charges for preventing the evils where they are ascribable to physical causes (Campbell 1984).

The National Board of Health was established in 1848.

The principle of equal distribution of medical care services was accepted by the British Medical Association long before the Beveridge Report that led to the establishment of the National Health Service (Campbell 1984). This is perhaps not surprising because one of the main assumptions in the National Health Act, Section 1, is that 'a comprehensive national health service will ensure that for every citizen there is available whatever medical treatment he requires, in whatever form he requires it' (Campbell 1984). Here the assumption is patient based, rights based and consistent with the post World War II ideal of a society designed to protect individuals from harm. As such it appeals to the physician's traditional duty to those in need.

In the first part of this century progress was made in expanding the participation and entitlement of citizens for self-determination. The gross violation of human rights committed by Nazi physicians shocked the medical profession into a reformulation of its social contract and an examination of the ethical bases of its practice. The result was a strong restatement of the Hippocratic patient first principles. The World Medical Association issued a modern Hippocratic Oath, the Declaration of Geneva, and in the International Code of Medical Ethics laid down its commitment to both physician and patient autonomy. In a sense the profession was picking up where it left off, at the time of Percival, the Enlightenment values and natural rights of all persons.

Given the World War II experience and the profession's struggle with the doctrine of informed consent, it is difficult for physicians to agree to health economists' requests that they attend to the interests of society as well as those of their individual patients.

They are, however, aware of the cost implications of their work—every journal for the past 15 years has published increasing numbers of articles about health economics concerns and theory, technology evaluation, new forms of organizing the delivery of medical services, team care, and a large bowl of alphabet soup with HMOs, DRGs, PSROs, CONs to name but a few eponyms. National and international meetings are held for ordinary practitioners and experts alike, and we have all learned to watch the GNP percentages like fever curves.

Most medical associations have committees on social security matters, but the only formal ethical declaration stating the position of the profession is the Declaration of Copenhagen on Health Care Costs issued by the Standing Committee of Physicians to the Common Market in 1979. This document (attached as an appendix) clearly delimits direct physician responsibility to patient care. Doctors will contibute their medical knowledge to health economists and other planners but they see their subject domain as different. They use different concepts to analyse the same problem, have different approaches and conclusions. They agree to co-operate with authorities in studying the problem but feel duty bound to speak up when service levels fall below those for which physicians will accept responsibility for patient care. The ten countries' national medical associations that signed the Declaration of Copenhagen represent different systems of providing medical services, which in turn reflect different views of medical services as facilitating personal autonomy for the patient, justice as fairness, or equity issues. This is what they could agree on by consensus.

One of the recurring questions that physicians asked was 'how do health economists justify their request to physicians on efficiency?' It might be useful to discuss this question in view of the setting of how these doctors work. They provide medical services, some curative and some preventive, to identifiable human beings in a process that requires trust and respect for the very vulnerability of the bodies of the said people. The ethical concepts that physicians bring to their work have evolved as an entwinement of business concerns and patient priority in a long and slow process.

If health economics is to challenge Hippocrates, and if it is to receive co-operation from the medical profession in this challenge, it must do so in a way that does not conflict with the historically and conceptually central patient-priority ethic of medicine. Physicians have only in the last 100 years freed themselves from a patronage system of practice and in the process have emphasized the importance of clinical autonomy for the good of patients. The question is, whether they should as a modern profession accept a new form of patronage practice—the state—and integrate the goal of efficiency without working out how this can be integrated with the commitment to individualized patient care.

6.4. Epilogue

As we have seen, the nature of medicine and of medical ethics have changed through time partly at least as a result of changing economic circumstances of the medical profession and of the organization of health care. The concern about the relationship between medical ethics and economics is not new.

But, moving away from a longitudinal analysis through time, can we learn anything from cross-sectional comparisons across different countries with different methods of financing health care and remunerating doctors? This was a theme which arose on several occasions at the workshop itself. Yet it is clear that while history would suggest to us that economic organization and conditions do influence medical ethics, there is little research to date which has looked at this question across different countries today.

How does an NHS type system affect medical ethics and medical ethical codes? In terms of medical ethics, does it make any difference if doctors are salaried or paid on a fee-per-item-of-service basis? There is evidence that they behave differently under the two systems. Is it then possible that in both instances they are doing their best for their patients?

Has the introduction of DRGs (diagnostic related groups) influenced medical conduct and/or medical ethics? If doctors have to operate within fixed budgets how does that affect their clinicial decision making and is this acceptable within the terms of the Copenhagen declaration quoted at the start of this chapter?

These are questions that need answers, particularly as the historical perspective would suggest that these different economic arrangements may well have a bearing on medical ethics. Here perhaps is the basis for some future workshop on medical ethics and economics.

Appendix to Chapter 6

DECLARATION ON HEALTH CARE COSTS

adopted at Copenhagen, 1978

The Standing Committee of Doctors of the EEC is highly conscious of the financial repercussions associated with the increase in the cost of health care. However, it observes that if health expenses are growing more rapidly than the national revenues of each member state, the basic reasons for this are the following:

— Demographic change and a noticeable increase in the number of elderly people.
— Scientific progress and the diffusion of technical progress in every region of all the member states: the prodigious leap forward in techniques has permitted a considerable improvement in investigative procedures and treatment; this has made curable diseases which were formerly inevitably fatal; it has enabled handicapped people to live, it allows the treatment of conditions previously considered fatal. It contributes to change patterns of illness. Morbidity is evolving, but not diminishing.
— Cultural progress: this has provoked an increased demand for care in relation to the standard of education and of information of the population, and it has indisputably lowered the threshold of tolerance of disease.
— Finally, if the development of social institutions has enabled every family budget to meet its health care needs, these were not created by it.

In 1967, the organizations of the Standing Committee drew up and adopted unanimously a Declaration by the Doctors of the European Economic Community on the subject of professional practice within the Community, Article 57–3 of the Treaty of Rome.

In this declaration . . . the doctors of the EEC underlined the fundamental principles of the duties of the doctor and also of the state in a modern society corresponding to the level of industrialization and expansion of the European Economic Community. The conclusion of the declaration was the following:

Technical progress, the basis of our industrial civilisation, and economic expansion which is the fruit of it, have the natural result, due in particular to a policy on health, of aiding the physical and spiritual development of man and of all men.

The doctors of the European Economic Community do not however, consider that everything is possible in our modern society and that the profession can remain indifferent to the repercussions of the cost of health care on the economics of the State. They believe it is their duty to collaborate in researching measures which aim at a better use and rationalization of resources set aside for health care, on the express condition that in all circumstances the freedom of prescription of the doctor, the natural defender of every patient, should be respected.

Indeed, the doctor cannot, in the context of an individual case, place the interests of society above those of the individual. Medicine is impossible without mutual confidence between the doctor and his patient. This confidence is based on fundamental freedoms: for the patient, the freedom to choose his doctor, and for the latter, the freedom to choose the necessary investigative and therapeutic methods. This confidence, which is indispensable, ceases to exist when confidentiality is not scrupulously respected and guaranteed.

As economic responsibilities are the province of political power, doctors cannot, without imperilling the technical and moral independence vital for the practice of their profession, associate themselves with the economic and political decisions which are taken by the public authorities with regard to the budget allocated to health care.

But expert advice must be taken before those concerned decide, and at this stage the medical profession intends to be consulted. Equally, when the decision has been taken, the medical profession intends to make known its assessment of the consequences of these choices.

The medical profession is prepared to assume the responsibility of advising those who must ensure the best use of the resources of health insurance and of the budget allocated to health care and, in this regard also, it reserves the right to publish its remarks and comments on the choices thus made.

Furthermore, the Standing Committee of Doctors of the European Economic Community alerts governments to the dangerous consequences of decisions taken on purely economic grounds. It recalls that a medical policy cannot be founded simply on the criterion of prolonging the span of life, but above all it should evaluate the quality of life that medicine can give to the sick, the handicapped, the chronically ill, and the aged.

The function of medicine is to participate, now and in the future, in the betterment of the life of man and society. The medical profession is ready to appeal to the population of all the member states so that this fundamental aim should be respected by the political powers of the states.

References

Aristotle (translated by Terence Irwin). (Cited from 1985 edition.) *Nicomachean ethics* 1105 a 26ff. Hackett Publishing Co., Indianapolis, Indiana.

Aristotle, *Politics* 1260 a 36–62. The Great Books Series, Vol. 9. Encyclopedia Britannica, Chicago.

Campbell, A. (1984). *Moral dilemmas in medicine*. Churchill Livingstone, Edinburgh, p. 47.

Cicero (translated by W. Miller). (Cited from 1913 edition.) *De officiis* (On duties). The Loeb Classical Library. Harvard University Press, Cambridge, Massachusetts.

Edelstein, L. (1967a). Ethics of the Greek physician. In A. Temkin and C. L. Temkin (ed.) *Ancient medicine*, Johns Hopkins Press, Baltimore. pp. 392, 401.

Edelstein, L. (1967b). The oath. In A. Temkin and C. L. Temkin (ed.). *Ancient medicine*. Johns Hopkins Press, Baltimore. p. 323.

Galdston, I. (1940). Humanism and public health. *Bulletin of Historical Medicine*, **8**, 1032.

Galen (translated by Dr Ch. Daremberg). (Cited from 1851 edition.) *Que le bon medecin est philosophe* (essay: That the best physician is also a philosopher). J. B. Baillière, Paris.

Herzlich, C. (1982). The evolution of relations between French physicians and the state from 1880–1980. *Sociology of Health and Illness*, **4**, 241–53.

Hippocrates (translated by W. H. Jones). (Cited from 1962 edition.) Vol. 2 *The arts*, p. 193. The Loeb Classical Library. Harvard University Press, Cambridge, Massachusetts.

Ibid. Vol. 2 *On decorum*, pp. 267–303.

Ibid. Vol. 2 *On the physician*, p. 303–15.

Ibid. Vol. 1 *Precepts*, pp. 319, 321.

Holloway, S. W. F. (1964). Medical education in England, 1830–1858: a sociological analysis. *History*, **XLIX**, 320.

Jewson, N. (1976). The disappearance of the sick-man from medical cosmology 1770–1870. *Sociology*, **10**, 225–44.

Leake, C. D. (1927). *Percival's medical ethics*. Johns Hopkins Press, Baltimore. p. 36.

Maas, P. L. and Oliver, J. (1939). An ancient poem on the duties of a physician. *Bulletin of Historical Medicine* **7**, 315.

Norden, E. (1905). De officiis judicis. *Hermes Zeitschrift für Klassische Philogie* **40**, 512. Berlin, 1866.

Percival, T. (1803; cited from 1975 reprint.) *Medical ethics: or a code of institutes and precepts. Adapted to the professional conduct of physicians and surgeons*. J. Johnson and R. Bickerstaff, London. Reprinted by R. E. Kreifer Pub. Co., Huntington, NY.

Percival, T. (1803). Of professional conduct. In W. J. Curran (ed.) (1977) *Ethics in medicine* MIT Press, Cambridge. pp. 18–25.

Plato (translated by G. M. A. Grube). (Cited from 1981 edition.) *Republic*, Book 1, 346 E–347 A. Pan Books, London.

Pseudegraphic Platonic dialogue. (Cited from 1923 edition.) *Eryxias* 393A and 394E. In *Greek economics* (ed. M. L. W. Laistner), p. xxviii. J. M. Dent and Sons, London.

Rossel, P. (1979). *Medicinsk etik*, GEC Gad, Copenhagen. p. 37.

Scribonius. (Cited from 1950 source.) In Karl Deichgräber *Professio medicie zum vorwort des Scribonius Largus*, p. 221. Abh. Akad. Geistes-u. Socialwissklasse No. 9.

Starr, P. (1977). Medicine, economy and society in nineteenth century America. In Branca P. (ed.) *The medicine show*. Science History Pub., New York. p. 51.

Temkin, O. (1949). Changing concepts of the relation of medicine to society: In early history. In I. Galdston *Social medicine: its derivation and objectives*, pp. 3–12. Commonwealth Fund, New York.

Waddington, I. (1984a). *The medical profession in the industrial revolution*. Gill and Macmillan, Dublin.

Waddington, I. (1984b). Note, Henk Heijnen, re. Plattelandschirufgijns in De 17e en 18e Eeuw, Dirk Jan Baptisk Ringoir *The medical profession in the industrial revolution*. Gill and Macmillan, Dublin. p. 190. For UK and USA see Ch. 9.

Waddington, I. (1984c). Adam Smith's letter to William Cullen. *The medical profession in the industrial revolution*. Gill and Macmillan, Dublin. p. 141.

7

Medical ethics and economics in clinical decision making

BRYAN JENNETT

Summary

Clinicians may claim to see a conflict between ethics and economics in some circumstances when this is a false antithesis. When all the evidence is that a patient's condition is beyond influence it is appropriate to withhold or to withdraw therapeutic technology. In patients too mildly affected to justify expensive investigation or treatment the lack of benefit is less definite and the decision whether the possible marginal benefit justifies the financial outlay or the intangible personal costs to the patient rests on a value judgement. To use certain technologies in either of these circumstances may infringe the ethical principle of non-maleficence, because the patient is exposed to inconvenience, discomfort, indignity, or hazard, without expectation of benefit. It may conflict also with the principle of allocative justice because when resources are restricted the decision to use an expensive intervention for a patient too ill to benefit inevitably deprives another less severely affected patient of the opportunity to benefit.

A more genuine dilemma arises when a choice has to be made between alternative methods of management that differ greatly in their costs—financial and personal. If the more costly is also the more effective then some doctors would hold that economic considerations should not influence their choice. In such a situation decisions should, however, depend on explicit exploration of the trade-offs before a value judgement is made about whether the benefits of the more expensive method are worth the extra cost.

Doctors wishing to avoid making a decision to withhold or withdraw investigative or therapeutic technologies sometimes plead an ethical dilemma based on the supposed uncertainty of the likelihood of benefit. As data banks and prognostic models become available for an increasing number of conditions this excuse is less often valid. However, some doctors' reaction to such data is to express unwillingness to act unless calculated probabilities are 100 per cent certain. Other doctors declare that even if probabilities of benefit could be reliably estimated the doctor's role as patient's advocate would be subverted by considering either these or economic considerations when making decisions about management. It is inappropriate use of technologies that no country can afford for economic reasons, nor should tolerate on humanitarian grounds.

Clinicians are uncertain about the meaning of the terms cost-effective and cost-benefit. They often suspect that they are cloaks for cuts in services or for savings in expenditure. Their shield against these threatening intruders is another much misunderstood word—ethics. They suppose that invoking ethics will ensure that clinical freedom remains sacrosanct, which in turn appears to empower clinicians to act as patient's advocates. They can then seek to ensure that *their* patients have access to all possible services, regardless of need or expectation of benefit relative to the patients of other specialists   (Jennett 1984a).

The divergence between what is good for the patient and what is efficient for society as a whole is a key element in current concerns over health-care spending ... The pressure to be more economical in the provision of care will force physicians to make decisions that are contrary to the best interests of individual patients   (Fuchs 1984).

The above quotations indicate the potential for conflict between doctors and economists and suggest that the field of ethics could become the battleground. On the other hand, ethics could become common ground for clinicians and economists—to the benefit of both individual patients and of society. As others in this volume point out there has been a change in the role of ethics in medicine in recent years. Previously it was largely to do with etiquette, concerned with codes of conduct between one doctor and another within the profession. In so far as ethics addressed relationships between the profession corporate and the public as a whole the focus was on protectionism for the profession in the name of protecting the public from quacks.

Contact between doctors and patients used to be largely on a one-to-one basis but doctors could seldom influence the outcome of illness. Recent developments have now made it possible to alter significantly what happens to many patients who have illness that threatens life or seriously impairs its quality. This often involves the use of complex technologies that depend on teams of skilled staff centred in hospitals. Doctors now comprise less than 10 per cent of health care workers in hospital compared with 30 per cent at the turn of the century. However, it is doctors who decide on the deployment of these expensive resources. Moreover that expense is now met by society as a whole rather than by sick individuals and their families. The public is therefore increasingly concerned that its health care resources are wisely used.

Apart from financial burdens there are often personal costs to be paid—in the risks, discomfort, and indignity often associated with technological interventions. Neither the financial cost nor these personal burdens are justified unless there is a reasonable probability that the patient will benefit. The possibility of expensively extending life of poor quality therefore poses a dilemma that has both ethical and resource dimensions. A major concern of medical ethics today is with relationships between doctors and patients in situations of this kind.

In Britain health care costs are fixed and the concern about technology is mainly about how best to use these within an ethical framework of personal and social justice. In the US the problem is seen primarily as one of budget deficit and secondly as one that raises social issues. Under the title 'Medicine versus economics' an American health economist recently focused on the potential of modern technology to make dying an expensive business, with scope for almost unlimited expenditure before reaching the traditional 'do no harm' stopping point (Thurow 1985).

'Technology' dominates all these discussions. I shall deal with clinical decision making in the field of high technology because this illustrates most starkly the conflict between ethics and economics at the bedside. Although many of the recent technological developments in medicine have been in radiology and the diagnostic laboratory I shall focus on therapeutic technologies because the relationship between intervention and patient benefit is more direct than it is with diagnostic technology. In therapy the agency relationship referred to by Mooney and McGuire (Chapter 2) is vital—but this is complicated by doctors having to be double agents in more ways than one. The patient expects the doctor to act as an adviser and advocate, but the doctor has also to be the gatekeeper to the health care resources of society. The doctor is also a key actor in moral dilemmas at both personal and societal levels—for example, in certain aspects of reproduction and in the management of the hopelessly ill.

What patients want from their doctors therefore is information, advice, and access to health care resources in general and in particular to the technical skills of the specialist team relevant to their present illness. What society wants from its doctors is that avoidable mortality and morbidity should be minimized by the prevention and cure of disease, and when this ideal cannot be met that doctors should strive to maximize quality of life by palliative measures. But society also wishes its doctors to use its health care resources wisely and economically, as well as to maintain public morale and morals both by these activities and by acting appropriately in moral dilemmas.

7.1. Ethics and economics in deciding about the use of therapeutic technologies

Therapeutic technologies are rationed most of the time almost everywhere so that decisions have to be made about when to initiate or to discontinue various measures in individual patients. The use of isolated items of expensive equipment is less important than the deployment of technological packages that have high staffing costs (e.g. intensive care and major surgery). Decisions of this kind about individual patients are more readily and more consistently made when the most appropriate way to deal with commonly occurring clinical problems has already been agreed and when such a prior consensus has taken account both of individualistic and of societal ethical principles. What matters for patients are beneficence, non-maleficence, and respect for their autonomy. For society the concern is that the distribution of resources and access to necessary services should be equitable; if opportunity costs are too high the ethical principle of allocative justice is infringed. When decisions are made at the bedside about patients it is the individualistic ethic that has to predominate. But some consideration can be given to the welfare of society as a whole even in such circumstances if such decisions are influenced by guidelines that have already been agreed. For when guidelines are drawn up outside the context of an individual patient the opportunity costs involved in treating various different kinds of patients can legitimately be taken in account. This leaves the clinician to decide how these guidelines apply to various patients.

Quite often when clinicians claim to see a conflict between ethics and economics this can be a false antithesis, because in some cases the limitation on the use of a given technology that economics demands would also be in the patient's best interest. These are mostly situations in which the use of a technology is either unnecessary or likely to be unsuccessful. The expected benefit is then so marginal that it justifies neither the financial outlay nor the intangible personal costs to the patient and his family. Exposing a patient unjustifiably to the inconvenience, discomfort, indignity, or hazard of an intervention that produces no significant benefit is bad ethics as well as bad economics. There would be fewer accusations that high technology is either inhumane or too costly if greater care were taken not to use it unnecessarily on patients who were too mildly affected to justify it, or unsuccessfully on those who were too badly affected to benefit. This implies application of the principle of triage that was employed by Napoleon's medical officers and by the US military in Vietnam when dealing with mass casualties. This ensures that the limited medical resources available are used for those whose outcome depends on treatment and are not wasted on those unlikely to benefit.

The problem is that doctors often disagree about which patients fall into each of these three categories. These differences in medical opinion are probably a more important cause of the geographical variations in the use of certain technologies than are differences in available resources. For such variations are found not only between countries but within one nation. They are striking even in Britain where resources are supposedly distributed equitably according to population-based formulae. Moreover such variations apply to procedures of acknowledged effectiveness such as cardiac surgery and renal dialysis and also to some procedures that are not subject to restraint by limited resources.

A striking variation is the tenfold difference between the number of intensive care beds in the US and the UK, which alone accounts for more than half the discrepancy in hospital expenditure on health care between the two countries, according to the study of Aaron and Schwartz (1984).

7.2. Unnecessary use of intensive care in the US

Many patients in intensive care units (ICUs) in America do not need the expensive skills and technologies that these units provide. In one study of general ICUs 70 per cent of patients were not critically ill and less than 10 per cent ever needed an intervention (Thibault *et al.* 1980). In some coronary care units half the patients proved not to have a heart attack, having been admitted only because of suspicious chest pain. In some places large numbers of patients are routinely transferred to intensive care after major surgery but very few ever develop complications. These admissions are supposedly justified by a 'safety first' philosophy. But apart from costing three to four times more per diem there are undesirable aspects of intensive care for the patient who is not critically ill. He is subject to frequent disturbance, to 24-hour activity and light, to social deprivation, and to witnessing the plight of very sick patients around him. He is also exposed to the risks of infection and of invasive monitoring. Better prognostic indices are needed to identify which patients are at high enough risk to justify admission to an ICU.

7.3. Unsuccessful treatment in intensive care units

Many patients in American ICUs are terminally ill (Bayer *et al.* 1983). Some have developed a critical episode at the end of chronic progressive disease; a few were previously healthy but have suffered an overwhelming crisis; many are elderly. For several conditions there are now reliable prognostic data based on severity of illness and age that can identify patients for whom survival of acceptable quality and reasonable duration is not possible no matter how much is done for them. In some cases a confident prognosis can be made only after observing the response to intensive monitoring and treatment over several hours. The problem then is to withdraw treatment that has already been started—because doctors and nurses are by then often caught in a cycle of commitment (Jennett 1984b). But unless there are agreed rules for discontinuing treatment there may be reluctance to embark on measures that might bring benefit—because of the fear that a prolonged period of futile treatment may then be inevitable.

7.4. The difficulty of saying no to the hopelessly ill

A study of the reactions of physicians to the rationing of intensive care in America showed a willingness to exclude patients identified as too mildly affected to benefit, but great reluctance to withhold or withdraw treatment from the hopelessly ill (Singer *et al*. 1983; Knaus 1986). Yet these latter patients are not only more expensive but they and their families have more to lose if life-extending measures are used inappropriately. In that economic and ethical requirements coincide in such cases it should be relatively easy to decide to limit treatment. In practice doctors tend to respond to imperatives to inappropriate action when they are managing acutely ill patients (Jennett 1986). These include the natural wish to respond to serious disease or distressing symptoms, as well as to the expectations of the patient and his family and of other doctors and of nurses that something active will be done. There is also sometimes the fear that legal action may by prompted by organizations that encourage the reporting of doctors who are withdrawing or withholding treatment. Lack of confidence about the hopelessness of the prognosis frequently contributes to indecisive or inappropriate action in such circumstances.

In spite of these constraints there are now increasing numbers of reports from the US about limiting treatment. Some focus on 'do not resuscitate' (DNR) orders but others recognize a range of levels of care as various measures are withheld or discontinued. These include active interventions such as major surgery, dialysis, or cancer chemotherapy as well as the use of antibiotics for newly developing infections. There is now open discussion about withholding even nutrition and fluid from patients in a stable state who are not sentient and cannot recover awareness but who if diligently nursed can survive for years in 'a state worse than death' (i.e. the vegetative state).

Ethical reasons for limiting treatment are to avoid prolonging the process of dying and to accede to the wishes of the patient. There is still some controversy about the extent to which patients should be required or invited to express preferences for and against life-extending treatment when they have not already made a declaration or living will. Although ethical issues dominate there are considerable economic implications of limiting care. Many patients who eventually have DNR orders have already attracted an undue proportion of resources before treatment is limited. The earlier after admission to intensive care that DNR orders are issued the more significant is the saving of resources (Zimmerman *et al*. 1986).

An American court recently criticized an ICU that had failed to establish arrangements to ensure that a hopeless patient already under treatment would give way to a newcomer whose expectation of benefit was much greater (Engelhardt and Rie 1986). The report of that case suggested that an 'entitlement index' might facilitate choices between patients competing for costly technologies. This would be based on estimates of the probability of benefit—of extending life of reasonable quality for a significant period of time. This implies that such limitation may be appropriate not only for patients who are inevitably dying but also for some who could survive for a time but with life of very poor quality. Indeed in one study only 39 per cent of DNR orders were for patients considered to be in a terminal condition.

7.5. Rationing when benefits and costs have to be balanced

Doctors therefore often find it difficult to ration rationally even in situations where to do so is manifestly in the best interests both of the individual patient and of society. Given that this is so the prospect is not good for wise choices being made between alternative treatments each of which promises some benefit but that have different costs. Sometimes the less costly method is also the more beneficial—for example kidney transplantation compared with dialysis for the treatment of renal failure. It might therefore seem obvious that the right policy would be to maximize the proportion of patients whose renal replacement is by transplantation. Yet there are wide variations in practice between different countries; the proportion of patients on renal replacement therapy who are treated by transplantation is twice as great in Britain as in the US.

It is when the more beneficial method is also the more costly that a genuine conflict between ethics and economics can arise. How the trade-offs between marginal benefits and marginal costs are viewed in various circumstances is a matter of value judgement. Clinical necessity requires that such judgements be made even when the data available about benefits and costs are inadequate. Consequently decisions about the use of expensive therapies are often based more on opinion than on weighing evidence. There is urgent need for more information about the assessment of technologies—both their clinical effectiveness and their economic implications. Partly this involves considering how to undertake economic appraisal. I shall limit myself to the need for clinicians to undertake more stringent evaluation of their technologies—both new and old. In many ways it is more important to review established techniques because these are already widely available and used. Moreover their evaluation may be facilitated by the abundance of data about their use; synthesis of these data may make formal trials unnecessary or it may allow these to be limited to certain unresolved issues.

As well as arguments about which technologies produce how much benefit in which patients there are controversies about how technologies are best assessed. No one method of assessment is appropriate in all circumstances—drugs, diagnostic equipment, surgery, and technological packages each present different problems. Moreover assessment is a costly business that may itself be a waste of resources unless it is carried out economically and it subsequently has an influence on the provision and use of the technology in question.

There are some commentators for whom the only acceptable evidence is a randomized control trial (RCT). Like some of those technologists whom they wish to put on trial for promoting technologies that allegedly have been inadequately evaluated some of these evaluators are themselves uncritical champions for their own product. The purpose of an RCT is to discover the influence and outcome of different means of management by comparing what happens to groups of patients differently treated but whose outcome was expected to be similar had they been treated in the same way. An alternative approach is to evolve a reliable prognostic model based on sound statistical analysis of data from large numbers of patients that have been collected prospectively according to a rigorous protocol. An example is the Glasgow-based international data bank of severe head injuries which now has in its computer details of 2500 patients from Glasgow, from two centres in the Netherlands, and from two in California. Wide variations were found between the methods of management used in different centres and these differences were utilized to compare the influence of certain aspects of management on outcome. A predictive model was evolved based on various aspects of severity of injury and on the patient's age. When the data collected from patients in one centre were used to predict outcome in patients elsewhere whose treatment was different there was a close correspondence between the number of deaths that was predicted and the number that actually occurred (Murray 1986; Jennett 1987). A similar technique was later used by Knaus to compare the influence on outcome of the different regimes of management used in general ICUs in the US and in France (Knaus *et al.* 1982).

It has been said that prognosis is the most essential skill in medicine. When doctors could do little to influence the course of an illness their reputations rested largely on their ability to predict its outcome. That is still important nowadays in the many conditions that have not yet yielded to efforts at therapy. But when there are potentially useful therapies prognosis is also important—because prognostic uncertainty is the commonest excuse for using them inappropriately. Prognostic models are also useful for assessing the relative values of alternative technologies and for decision making about their use for individual patients. These are examples of the expert systems discussed by Hucklenbroich (Chapter 8).

In practice few technologies prove never to be useful while none is always useful—in particular when used on the 'wrong' patients (those too mildly affected to need it or those too severely affected to benefit). The aim of assessment is to discover for each technology the sliding scale of value in terms of benefits and burdens for various types of patients and so to define the limits of appropriate use. Occasionally a widely used technology is shown to be of little or no use, as when the trial of transcranial bypass surgery for patients at risk from stroke showed no benefit in any of several subsets of 1377 patients studied (EC/IC Bypass Study Group 1985). That particular exercise in technology assessment indicates the timescale and cost of evaluation. It took 8 years to complete and it was not until 18 years after this operation had been introduced that it was shown to be of no value. Although the trial cost $9m it was estimated that $11m were saved during the course of the study because half the patients were randomized to a much less costly alternative treatment than surgery. This investment in evaluation promises to yield an annual dividend of some $30m in the US—provided that surgeons do alter their practice by abandoning this ineffective operation.

It is, however, one thing to demonstrate the appropriate use of a technology and another to persuade doctors on a large scale to adjust their practice accordingly. The imperatives already listed as inclining doctors to employ useless treatment for hopeless patients apply even more strongly when there is a question of some benefit for some patients. One approach would be to organize consensus conferences to produce a majority view among experts and others. The findings of such meetings could then be translated by a specialist society into practical guidelines on a national scale which could then be modified according to local circumstances and the views of doctors within an institution. Not all doctors are likely to agree to abide by such guidelines but even if the majority of doctors were to make their decisions in accordance with the best data available then good practice would soon become common practice. To expect it to become universal is to ask too much of a profession that prides itself on the freedom of clinicians to decide what they think is best for their patient—even when they are wrong.

What is needed is for doctors to accept that part of good practice is that it should be economic practice. This is where the quality-adjusted life-year (QALY) can prove a useful tool for comparing the costs and benefits of technologies used for different diseases as well as for showing the range of trade-offs between different managements and types of patient with the same condition. The QALY depends on estimates of quality of life based on the views of patients and families as well as of doctors and others involved in the personal care of sick people. It also takes account of data about the expected duration of life with and without certain interventions. For example, successful coronary artery bypass may gain several QALYs for a severely affected patient with heart disease who not only has painful angina but is likely to have only a short survival without surgery (Williams 1985). By contrast a mildly affected patient gains little—but it costs just as much for the treatment and the risks from the operation are similar. The cost per QALY is therefore much higher when such a patient is submitted to surgery.

The QALY makes it possible to compare different means of treating one condition (e.g. renal failure) and also of extending life of quality by technological interventions for different conditions (e.g. dialysis v. heart transplant v. coronary artery surgery). It has hitherto been difficult to compare the relative worthwhileness of treating different conditions, but this method allows a cost–benefit approach that compares ends as well as means. This may go some way to reducing the influence of competing advocates who have so far depended on special pleading for dread diseases such as cancer or heart attacks, or for vulnerable or worthy types of patient. The latter include children, pregnant women, parents, bread winners and the elderly—each of whom can for different reasons be portrayed as more 'deserving' than others. That is not to say that estimating the monetary value of the benefits gained by alternative treatments eliminates value judgements about the relative merits of different strategies of resource allocation and use. But it does indicate to the utilitarian what trade-offs are at stake before deciding how much attention to pay to subjective comparisons when making choices in the use of technology, whether between groups of patients with different disease, or between individuals with the same condition who vary in age and severity of illness.

7.6.   Further Anglo-American comparisons

It might seem obvious that the way to ration health care would be to choose to do what will most probably produce the most benefit. However, when a medical journal published two papers by health economists recommending this utilitarian approach (Fuchs 1984; Thurow 1984) an American physician commented that it was dangerous to conserve resources by using the probability of success to choose between patients (Levinsky 1984). He regarded the doctor's role as advocate for his patient to be subverted by what he denigrated as 'probabilistic practice'. He was even suspicious of identifying some patients as being hopelessly ill. What was encouraging was that all the letters published by that journal after these three papers disagreed with the doctor and supported the arguments of the economists. Yet all of these letters were written by doctors.

A comparison of the use of ten technologies in UK and US around 1980 revealed very uneven differences (Aaron and Schwartz 1984). Although health care spending was about four times as great per capita in the US there were several technologies that were used equally frequently in the two countries. These included radiotherapy and chemotherapy for potentially curable cancer, renal and bone marrow transplantation, and the treatment of haemophilia with blood products. What characterizes all of these therapies is their acknowledged benefit to most patients who receive them. By contrast in America many diagnostic X-ray examinations were used twice as often as in the UK and twice as many films were used at each examination; CT scanners were six times more frequent and intensive care beds were ten times more frequent per million population. Chemotherapy for incurable cancer was used five times more often than in Britain.

Each of the therapies used at very different rates is of dubious benefit in many circumstances. It seems likely that the differences in their rates of use are mostly because they are often employed in the US in situations which British doctors would deem to be inappropriate (unnecessary or unsuccessful). There is moreover no evidence that the greater use of these technologies in the US is reflected in correspondingly better health. It is, however, often claimed by American commentators that the much lower use of renal replacement therapy and of coronary artery surgery in Britain indicates that many British patients are deprived of potential benefit. On the other hand there is little doubt that coronary surgery is frequently used in the US for patients with relatively mild disease whom British doctors would not consider for operation because this would not bring sufficient benefit to justify its use. However, the rates of use of these two technologies are coming closer together in the two countries as each acknowledges a degree of over and under-use respectively.

The same goes for several other surgical procedures that are carried out many times more often in the US. One is transcranial bypass in an effort to prevent stroke—which has already been described as having been shown to be of no benefit. Another is carotid endarterectomy, which is carried out on 100 000 patients a year in the US without there being any evidence that its capacity to reduce the risk of stroke is greater than the morbidity and mortality associated with the surgery. Neither of these operations is commonly carried out in UK.

There are many reasons why procedures of little or no proved benefit are used more frequently in the US. One commonly given reason is pressure for intervention on the part of patients and families—but this is often generated by physicians and surgeons offering unrealistic prospects. This highlights the difficulties in the way of respecting patient autonomy and allowing freedom of choice. For these ethical principles can benefit patients only if doctors provide patients with honest information about the relative burdens and benefits associated with alternative courses of action. That in turn is possible only if the various technologies have been adequately evaluated. In other words, technology assessment is a necessary prerequisite for the ethical use of technology (Jennett 1986). Only when it is known what the probabilities are can decisions be taken that are in the best interests of patients and of society, and in collaboration with informed patients. Without such data there is bound to be widespread use of technologies in circumstances that are inappropriate (Jennett 1986). Reasons why use may be deemed inappropriate are because it is unnecessary—because the patient is not seriously enough affected to need it, unsuccessful—because the patient is too badly affected to benefit, unsafe—because the risks outweigh the benefits, unkind—because the quality of life is unacceptable, or unwise—because it diverts resources from more beneficial activities in health care.

7.7. Conclusion

Ethical and economic issues should each be given their place when reaching decisions about the use of expensive clinical technologies. Often these two considerations will each point to the same decision because the course of action that is most justifiable on ethical grounds is also the most economic. When more costly therapy does offer a better prospect of benefit economic appraisal can help to quantify the marginal costs and benefits involved and this may help clinicians to make wiser and kinder decisions.

References

Aaron, H. J. and Schwartz, W. B. (1984). *The painful prescription: rationing hospital care*. The Brookings Institution, Washington DC.

Bayer, R., Callahan, D., Fletcher, J., Hodgson, T., Jennings, B., Monsees, D., Sieverts, S. and Veatch, R. (1983). The care of the terminally ill: morality and economics. *New England Journal of Medicine*, **309**, 1490–4.

EC/IC Bypass Study Group (1985). Failure of extracranial/intracranial bypass to reduce the risk of ischemic stroke: results of an international randomised trial. *New England Journal of Medicine* **313**, 1191–200.

Engelhardt, H. T., and Rie, M. A. (1986). Intensive care units, scarce resources and conflicting principles of justice. *Journal of the American Medical Association*, **255**, 150–64.

Fuchs, V. (1984). The 'rationing' of medical care. *New England Journal of Medicine*, **311**, 1572–3.

Jennett, B. (1984a). Economic appraisal. *British Medical Journal*, **288**, 1781–2.

Jennett, B. (1984b). Inappropriate use of intensive care. *British Medical Journal*, **289**, 1709–11.

Jennett, B. (1986). *High technology medicine—benefits and burdens*. (2nd edition). Oxford and New York, Oxford University Press.

Jennett, B. (1987). Assessment of a technological package using a predictive tool. *International Journal of Technology Assessment in Health Care*, in press.

Knaus, W. (1986). Rationing, justice and the American physician. *Journal of the American Medical Association*, **255**, 1176–7.

Knaus, W. A., Le Gall, J. R., Wagner, D. P., Draper, E. A., Loirat, P., Campos, R. A., Cullen, D. J., Kohles, M. K., Glaser, P., Granthil, C., Mercier, P., Nicolas, F., Nikki, P., Shim, B., Snyder, J. V., Wattel, J. V. and Zimmerman, J. E. (1982). A comparison of intensive care in the USA and France. *Lancet*, **2**, 642–6.

Levinsky, N. J. (1984). The doctor's master. *New England Journal of Medicine*, **311**, 1573–5.

Murray, G. D. (1986). Use of an international data bank to compare outcome following severe head injury in different centres. *Statistics in Medicine*, **5**, 103–12.

Singer, D. E., Carr, P. L., Mulley, A. G. and Thibault, G. E. (1983) Rationing intensive care: physician responses to a resource shortage. *New England Journal of Medicine*, **309**, 1155–60.

Thibault, G. E., Mulley, A. G. and Barnett, C. O. (1980). Medical intensive care: indications, interventions and outcome. *New England Journal of Medicine*, **302**, 938–42.

Thurow, L. C. (1984). Learning to say no. *New England Journal of Medicine*, **311**, 1569–72.

Thurow, L. C. (1985). Medicine versus economics. *New England Journal of Medicine*, **313**, 611–14.

Williams, A. (1985). Economics of coronary artery bypass grafting. *British Medical Journal*, **291**, 326–9.

Zimmerman, J. E., Knaus, W. A., Sharpe, S. M., Anderson, A. S., Draper, E. A. and Wagner, D. P. (1986). The use and implications of do not resuscitate orders in intensive care units. *Journal of the American Medical Association*, **255**, 351–6.

8

Medical ethics and economics in medical expert systems

PETER HUCKLENBROICH

Summary

Medical expert and consultation systems (MECS) are computer programs that are based on explicitly formulated medical knowledge and are devised to help the doctor in medical decision making. At the present stage of technological development it is possible to implement systems with large knowledge bases, such as an almost complete representation of clinical internal medicine, on relatively cheap office and personal computers. The introduction of such systems into medical practice will probably contribute to an increase in quality and economic efficiency by establishing a novel channel for the flow of integrated scientific information. In order to avoid ethical problems, the systems should give advice to the doctor (including on economic matters) but should not themselves make decisions on medical matters.

8.1. Introduction

The debate between representatives of health economics and of medical ethics, as documented in this volume, has led to an interesting impasse concerning the point at issue. It has not been possible to show convincingly that the ethical foundations of medical practice have to be altered in order to contain cost escalation or to promote economic efficiency in the health system (ten Have Chapter 3; Downie Chapter 4). At the same time, it has not been confirmed that it is sufficient to rely on what already exists regarding economic aspects in medical decision making (Gillon Chapter 9). Because the aims of cost containment and of economic efficiency are not in themselves controversial, the question of how to get closer to these aims becomes even more urgent. The proposal to exercise a global controlling effect through the macro-allocation of health care resources (Mooney and McGuire Chapter 2) not only encounters opposition from historically motivated ethico-political scruples (Sohl Chapter 6) but also comes up against the simple problem that the process of medical decision making is not clear and explicit enough about its presuppositions and potentialities to allow such global measures to be established. There is no appropriate mechanism to provide an overview of all the possible options and decisions in medical practice; further, no such mechanism renders possible such evaluation in terms of costs and benefits.

We are a long way from overcoming these difficulties. But currently there is a technological development that may allow some amelioration of these problems even at the present time and in the near future may lead to a radical change. I refer to the development of information technologies that has led to the origin of knowledge-based program systems for medicine (medical expert and consultation systems, MECS) and to the possibility of their widespread use and application by means of current micro and personal computers. This development, which has been taking place since the 1950s at an ever-increasing pace, has not yet been fully appreciated by its potential beneficiaries such as physicians and health insurers, but it is likely to attract their intention in the next few years. In what follows, I shall sketch the theoretical and technical foundations of these systems as well as the potential consequences of their application in terms of both economic and medico-ethical perspectives. It has to be emphasized that discussions of these matters have to be tentative and speculative for the present and will be supplemented and corrected by the experiences of the next few years.

8.2.   The development of computer science since 1940

The development of medical expert and consultation systems (MECS) must be viewed against the background of the development of computer science and technology. In the 1940s, the first digital computing machines (Zuse, Aiken, Eckert/Mauchley) and their basic theory (Turing, Wiener, Von Neumann) came into existence (Hanson 1982, 1984); and in the 1950s, the first universal programming languages were devised (FOR-TRAN, ALGOL-60) (Stoyan 1980). At the same time, the first attempts were made to utilize computers for clinical decision making (Puppe 1983; Reggia and Tuhrim 1985).

With the programming language LISP (McCarthy 1960, Stoyan and Görz 1984) symbolic computation became possible, leading to the development of artificial intelligence (AI) research in the 1960s (Stoyan 1980; Bibel and Siekmann 1982; Rich 1983). In 1969, Feigenbaum and his team built DENDRAL, the first expert system, operating in the area of chemical structural analysis (Feigenbaum *et al*. 1971). In the 1970s, quite a lot of medical expert systems were developed to run on mainframe computers. Among these are MYCIN, a consultation system for diagnosis and chemotherapy of infectious disease, CASNET, a system for diagnosis and treatment of glaucoma, the 'Digitalis Therapy Advisor', and the system

INTERNIST/CADUCEUS aimed at the whole field of diagnostics and differential diagnosis in internal medicine (Shortliffe 1976; Szolovits 1982; Buchanan and Shortliffe 1984; Clancey and Shortliffe 1984; Johnson and Keravnou 1985). At the same time, the programming language PROLOG was devised. This is capable of processing logically reconstructed knowledge formulated in the language of predicate logic (Kowalski 1979; Robinson 1979; Clocksin and Mellish 1984; Lloyd 1984).

At the end of the 1970s, the market for microcomputers was created by the micro-miniaturizing of integrated electronic circuits (microprocessors, microchips). In 1985, current 'personal computers' (PCs) attained the capacities of former 'minis'. In 1987, we can expect the 'mainframe PC' (32-bit microprocessors, optical storage media, laser technology). Practically all programming languages, including LISP and PROLOG, are available for PCs. The first expert system shells are already in the microcomputer market. It may be only a matter of a few months or years until most of the mainframe medical expert systems will be available for normal personal and office computers (Harmon and King 1986).

8.3. Methods of artificial intelligence

There are, of course, many ways of using a computer in the course of medical decision making, from its use as a kind of pocket (or desktop) calculator, through to its use as a storage medium and a device for statistical evaluation of patient data and clinical documentation, its use as a mathematical modelling device in studying complex (patho)physiological interrelations, and finally its use as a model of diagnostic and therapeutic reasoning itself. While noting the wide range of possibilities that have emerged since the 1950s, I shall confine myself to that branch of research which is based on an explicit representation of medical knowledge and on decision rules and heuristic procedures operating on this knowledge base. At present, this branch of research is usually regarded as one field of AI, called 'artificial intelligence in medicine' (AIM). I shall not discuss here the philosophical problems of AI raised by authors like Dreyfus (1972, 1985; Dreyfus and Dreyfus 1986) and Searle (1980, 1986), because it is only the application of some of the results of AI research in expert and consultation systems for medical practice that matters in the context of this chapter.

The difference between MECS and former systems for computer-aided clinical decision making not based on AI methods consists, essentially, of the existence of a knowledge base in the AI systems that is formed of explicitly formulated medical knowledge (so-called declarative representation of knowledge) and that can be displayed to the user like the contents of a medical textbook. Prior to this, in the non-AI systems, only the people capable of reading program code could extract the knowledge from the system ('procedural representation of knowledge'). However, in AI systems the knowledge base may be displayed in a commonly understandable language, for example as facts and rules formulated in a natural language like English or, at least, in a logically reconstructed natural language. This feature not only increases the intelligibility of the system for the user but also forms the decisive prerequisite for any attempt to transfer the entire body of medical knowledge, as it exists in the medical literature and 'in the heads of the experts', without any loss of information into the knowledge base of a program. Of course, this medical knowledge has to be adapted by a 'knowledge engineer' or, at least, must be formulated in a particular, fixed syntax, but these constraints are diminished by the progress in natural language processing and do not prevent the construction and maintenance of large and complex knowledge bases (Kohout and Bandler 1986).

A further advantage of the AI approach is that, whereas former systems had to work on the base of rigid and artificial oversimplifications of the clinical situation, in knowledge-based systems the precision of representation is dependent only on the explicitness and completeness of the reconstruction of knowledge. Anything that can be stated in natural language in a clear and unambiguous way may, in the long run, be transferred on to the knowledge base of an AI program. Therefore, the actual problems in the construction of medical (and other) expert systems do not stem from differences between man and machine in terms of knowledge representation but from the fact that making the knowledge explicit needs much more time and work than putting it into a suitable system. For this reason, time for constructing a 'complete' representation of medical knowledge is estimated to take more than a decade.

8.4. The functions of MECS

MECS have been designed for very different areas of problems with knowledge bases of very different sizes. It is therefore difficult to provide a unified account of their function. If we consider only systems that operate in dialogue with (medically competent) users, we find the following functional features in most systems:

— The system provides a capacity for reading in data and information about an individual patient or case by the user. This input function may be realized in different ways, for example by reading in a list of data and findings at the beginning of the session or by asking the user through a particular 'questionnaire' facility of the system. Normally, these possibilities are combined in some convenient way. If the system is part of a hospital information system or a system for documenting patient data, this information can be read in automatically from the main data base (Clayton *et al.* 1985).

— The system will process patient information on the basis of its knowledge base in order to achieve diagnostically and/or therapeutically relevant consequences. Depending on the particular design of the system, the questions and tasks solved may be internally generated or explicitly posed by the user. In most systems, the processing of knowledge and patient information involves various stages of logical reasoning and proof. Often the system includes a 'query-the-user' facility, that is, it is able to ask the user for information which is lacking and which is needed to solve a problem.

— The system may answer questions of the following types: Which diseases are possible causes of a given constellation of findings? By which measures is it possible to distinguish between different cases of a differential-diagnostic alternative? Which diagnostic and/or therapeutic measures are indicated or contraindicated in a given situation? Is the information sufficient for diagnosing? Can diagnosis D be confirmed or refuted on the basis of the findings? Are there differential-diagnostic possibilities that have been overlooked? Is there a therapeutic alternative to T? Also, a simple 'looking-up' function may be implemented, for example by answering questions such as: What is the symptomatology of disease D? Which groups of diseases are rendered probable by the sympton S? Which contraindications exist for drug M?

— During a consultation, the system may be asked to justify its answers, suggestions, and questions, that is, to display the responsible parts of its knowledge base. In this way, the 'decisions' of the system can be controlled and checked at any stage without knowledge of the internal structure of the program or of the programming language. This feature has proved to be particularly important in getting systems accepted by medically trained users.

— Usually, the system provides the possibility for extending or modifying its knowledge base by being able to process explicitly stated new facts, rules, or relations that are read in by the system and added to its body of knowledge. This may be done in order to integrate new results, to extend the domain of application, or to correct false or obsolete information. However, the general problem of integrating the growth or change of knowledge into a large and complex knowledge base leads to serious logical and philosophical problems. There must be an assurance that the modification does not render the whole system inconsistent, ambiguous, or indeterminate. Such conditions, which also have to be observed at the stage of the primary construction of the system and which cause much of the work connected with the development of correct systems, cannot be controlled sufficiently by automatic procedures at present. One way of solving this problem may be the explicit incorporation of meta-knowledge into the knowledge base, that is, the incorporation of logical and philosophical knowledge (in the sense of philosophy of science) and knowledge about the organization of the expert or consultation system itself (Hucklenbroich 1978, 1986a).

8.5. Strategies of basic and applied research in MECS

Medical knowledge as well as medical reasoning and decision-making strategies constjtute a very complex aggregation of very different conceptual strategies on distinct levels of abstraction, intuitive clearness, and precision, the intuitive management of which is an essential component of what is often called the art or artistic skill of medical practitioners. Among these skills are reasoning by appeal to spatial and morphological imaginations (impressions of space) and analogies, the use of concepts and intuitive knowledge of temporal processes and relations, reasoning by non-deterministic, fuzzy concepts and relations, flexibility in the correction and adaptation of given evaluations if new findings partially falsify previous information (the so-called non-linear reasoning), and a comprehensive common-sense and background knowledge about heterogeneous aspects of human life and its conditions. The reproduction of all these facilities of skilled physicians by computer programs is a task that, at the time present, has been solved to only a very small extent.

This means that research in the domain of medical expert systems or, more generally, of AI in medicine may be divided into two main areas. First, there is the area of research aimed at a perfect simulation or reproduction of the knowledge and the reasoning facilities of human experts in medicine. This research can only take the form of highly specialized basic research on the common foundations of logic, philosophy of science, and informatics (AI). The systems that are developed in this area must be viewed as scientific models, the primary role of which is to stimulate further research and not to guide medical practice as such. However, existing results and techniques are sufficient to create a second area of research, that of developing programs that are of use in the everyday practice of medicine. The aim of these program systems is not to imitate a physician but to complement his facilities through computerized, rapid access to large-scale knowledge bases. Systems of this type may be viewed as an 'intelligent library' which can automatically search for a piece of information, draw consequences from given information, and answer questions. Today's technology can realize systems of this type on current hardware like PCs or office computers because storage capacities and processing velocities are sufficient, thus making accessible these services to any physician in his own office or ward.

8.6. Economic consequences resulting from changes of information flow in medicine

There are several advantages in using knowledge-based systems in clinical practice. As a result of the enormous storage space available for the knowledge base, it is possible to obtain total availability, going far beyond the capacity of any individual physician, of all known clinical–nosological and pathological—pathophysiological information about findings, disease entities, and symptom–syndrome relationships, as well as about diagnostic and therapeutic indications. The automatic evaluation of the system's knowledge prevents errors as a result of overlooking, forgetting, incorrect reasoning, or personal bias. If the expert system is linked to a patient-administering or hospital information system, automatic checks of actual patient management and automatic evaluations of new diagnostic findings are possible.

Changes in the operation of a clinical ward or a physician's office resulting from the application of more or less comprehensive MECS, might include:

— No oversight of unexplained findings.
— No oversight of differential-diagnostic alternatives.
— No oversight of indicated measures.
— No unnecessary or duplicated clinical investigations.
— No loss of time in diagnosing rare syndromes, etc.
— More effective organization of the necessary examinations, measures, and counselling.
— Substitutes for unavailable counselling.
— Possibility of economic optimizing of diagnostic–therapeutic decisions.
— Early recognition of risk factors, premorbid changes, and pathological trends in long-term patient management.
— Clarification of the clinical decision process, in the individual case as well as generally.

The general and widespread introduction of expert and consultation systems into medical practice will cause a change in the flow of scientific information in medicine, in the sense that the locally available knowledge is increased. As a consequence, the quality of the knowledge-dependent components of medical decision making may also be increased. This effect can be represented in a flow chart of scientific information in medicine by introducing a second, 'integrated' channel for information flow parallel to the existing one (Table 8.1).

In this way the construction of MECS constitutes an integration of the results of research and communication at different levels, establishing a novel medium for information flow in medicine. The traditional media,

Peter Hucklenbroich

Table 8.1.

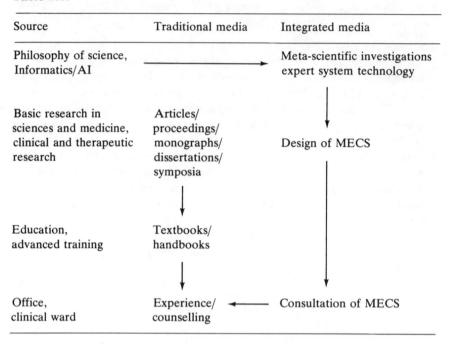

Source	Traditional media	Integrated media
Philosophy of science, Informatics/AI		Meta-scientific investigations expert system technology
Basic research in sciences and medicine, clinical and therapeutic research	Articles/ proceedings/ monographs/ dissertations/ symposia	Design of MECS
Education, advanced training	Textbooks/ handbooks	
Office, clinical ward	Experience/ counselling	Consultation of MECS

consisting of medical experience, oral communication, and print, such as books and journals, will not be replaced but complemented by this new medium.

The *economic* consequences of extending the medico-scientific information system in this way might best be described as the indirect consequences of condensing and increasing the information available locally (knowledge). The primary effect will be an increase in the quality of medical decision making. If diseases can be detected at an earlier stage, errors and superfluous measures avoided, and pressure arising from time constraints reduced, this will result in an increase of not only quality but also efficiency, in the economic sense, of the health care system. At the present time, it is difficult to make quantitative predictions about this effect, but no one would contest the considerable potential there is for improvements in this area. These improvements are not restricted to avoiding *medically* wrong decisions but may be extended to avoiding economically false or suboptimal decisions by extending the information delivered by the system to include economic aspects, for example through displaying the costs of the measures involved.

A further aspect that is economically relevant results from the fact that the possibility of consulting highly integrated expert knowledge at practically any point of the medical decision process will decrease the individual *risk* of decision making by linking the decision to collective experience. Of course, there will always remain a risk, but this link to collective experience accelerates the process of learning from others. This has always been a principle of scientific research and communication. Of course, there will be a potential problem regarding the responsibility for the correctness of a medical consultation system, just as it exists for the authors of scientific textbooks or other publications. This problem is discussed in the next section.

Finally, there must be the economic consideration of the costs of implementing medical consultation systems. First, the hardware costs will amount to £1000–8000 (3000–25 000 DM), if current personal or office computers are used. Second, there are the software costs, which, while more difficult to estimate, may roughly equal the hardware costs. Thus, the total costs will be £2000–15 000. However, in most cases a hardware system will already have been established for text processing, documentation, etc. This can be utilized and, consequently, only software costs would have to be met. Since updating is an important feature in medical expert systems, there may be a need for an annual update to the original system but the cost of this is likely to be relatively small. Taking all this together, the costs of implementing a medical expert or consultation system must be estimated to fall in the lower end of the spectrum for medical apparatus.

8.7. Ethics versus economics?

In characterizing the function of MECS above, I indicated that the systems display information or possibilities of choice, not that they themselves make decisions. Of course it is possible to build a system that automatically makes (medical) decisions according to an internal algorithm, for instance about the diagnostic strategy to take, or about diagnostic and therapeutic indications (Hucklenbroich 1986b). But such automatization carries the danger of being insufficiently controlled by the user and, possibly, of introducing wrong criteria and decisions, for example by being out of date. Moreover, it would be very difficult to find a general standard to evaluate every individual situation in medical practice. Therefore, a medical consultation system should display all possible choices and leave it to the user to make the final decision.

Even if the system is built in this way, there remains the problem that the builder has to decide which information is medically and scientifically correct, and which suggestions and indications are medically and ethically justified. Like the author of a scientific article or book, the expert system builder encounters the problem of responsibility for published knowledge. In the case of decisions regarding which measures are indicated in a particular situation, there remains the problem of reconciling ethical (in the 'individualistic' sense) and economic criteria, as it was formulated by Mooney and McGuire. The system builder must decide if a particular indication (say, a drug) should be included even if its costs are exorbitantly high and its benefits very low or doubtful. Of course it is possible to exclude all treatments of this kind completely from the knowledge base of the system or to rule them out by a suitable cost–benefit evaluation during the computation. Nevertheless, one should resist this tendency of macro-allocational control of consultation systems, because it might rightly be viewed as manipulation. Rather, one should use the abilities of such information systems positively by automatically displaying information about the costs and the possible success or benefit of a treatment that is under consideration (in so far as sound scientific information for this exists). In this way, the individual decision and cost–benefit evaluation is left to the physician and patient but is improved by becoming a kind of 'informed consent'. Thus, the transparency of the concrete medical situation may be increased also in this economic respect without being restricted in a dirigistic manner. Finally, in this way the introduction of medical expert and consultation systems may lead to a better basis for future discussions that aim at standardization and unification, as well as a critical evaluation, of contemporary rules and systems of medical indications.

References

Bibel, W. and Siekmann, J. H. (1982). *Künstliche Intelligenz*. Springer, Berlin.

Buchanan, B. G. and Shortliffe, E. H. (eds.) (1984) *Rule-based expert systems*. Addison-Wesley, Reading, Mass.

Clancey, W. J. and Shortliffe, E. H. (eds.) (1984). *Readings in medical artificial intelligence*. Addison-Wesley, Reading, Mass.

Clayton, P. D., Pryor, T. A., Gardner, R. M. and Warner, H. R. (1985). HELP—a medical information system which combines automated medical decision-making with clinical data review and administrative support. In Jesdinsky, H. J. and Trampisch, H. J. (eds.) *Prognose- und Entscheidungsfindung in der Medizin*. pp. 266–72. Springer, Berlin.

Clocksin, W. F. and Mellish, C. S. (1984). *Programming in Prolog*. Springer, Berlin.

Dreyfus, H. L. (1972). *What computers can't do: a critique of artificial intelligence*. Harper & Row, New York.

Dreyfus, H. L. (1985). *Die Grenzen künstlicher Intelligenz*. Athenäum, Königstein/Ts.

Dreyfus, H. L. and Dreyfus, S. E. (1986). *Mind over machine*. Free Press, New York.

Feigenbaum, E. A., Buchanan, B. G. and Lederberg, J. (1971). On generality and problem solving: a case study involving the DENDRAL program. In Meltzer B. and Michie, D. (eds.) *Machine Intelligence*, Vol. 6. pp. 165–90. American Elsevier, New York.

Hanson, D. (1982). *The new alchemists*. Little, Brown & Co., Boston.

Hanson, D. (1984). *Die Geschichte der Mikroelektronik*. Heyne, München.

Harmon, P. and King, D. (1986). *Expertensysteme in der Praxis*. Oldenbourg, München.

Hucklenbroich, P. (1978). *Theorie des Erkenntnisfortschritts*. Hain, Meisenheim.

Hucklenbroich, P. (1986a). *Organismus und Programm*. Diss. med., Münster.

Hucklenbroich, P. (1986b). Automatisation and responsibility. *Theoretical Medicine*, 7, 239–42.

Johnson, L. and Keravnou, E. T. (1985). *Expert Systems technology*. Abacus Press, Tunbridge Wells.

Kohout, L. J. and Bandler, W. (eds.) (1986). *Knowledge representation in medicine and clinical behavioural science*. Abacus Press, Cambridge, Mass.

Kowalski, R. (1979). *Logic for problem solving*. North Holland, New York.

Lloyd, J. W. (1984). *Foundations of logic programming*. Springer, Berlin.

McCarthy, J. (1960). Recursive functions of symbolic expressions and their computation by machine. Part 1. *Communications ACM*, 3, 185–95.

Puppe, B. (1983). *Die Entwicklung des Computereinsatzes in der medizinischen Diagnostik und MED1: Ein Expertensystem zur Brustschmerz-Diagnostik*. Diss. med., Freiburg.

Reggia, J. A. and Tuhrim, S. (eds.) (1985). *Computer-assisted medical decision making*. Springer, New York.

Rich, E. (1983). *Artificial intelligence*. McGraw-Hill, London.

Robinson, J. A. (1979). *Logic: form and function*. Edinburgh University Press, Edinburgh.

Searle, J. R. (1980). Minds, brains, and programs. *The Behavioral and Brain Sciences*, 3, 417–57.

Searle, J. R. (1986). *Geist, Hirn und Wissenschaft*. Suhrkamp, Frankfurt.

Shortliffe, E. H. (1976). *Computer-based medical consultations: MYCIN*. American Elsevier, New York.

Stoyan, H. (1980). *LISP—Anwendungsgebiete, Grundbegriffe, Geschichte*. Akademie-Verlag, Berlin.

Stoyan, H. and Görz, G. (1984). *LISP*. Springer, Berlin.

Szolovits, P. (ed.) (1982). *Artifical intelligence in medicine*. Westview Press, Boulder, Colo.

9

Ethics, economics, and general practice

RAANAN GILLON

Summary

This chapter argues that the common assumption that medical ethics and health economics based on welfare maximization are mutually incompatible is false and is based on simplistic stereotypes of both medical ethics and the ethics of health economics. In the first section examples from clinical practice are adduced to show that doctors do not in practice act as if they believe that 'the patient's interests always come first'—in practice they balance other moral considerations against their perceived special and strong but not absolute obligations to benefit their patients. Some presumably unacceptable results which would follow if doctors did act according to an absolute belief that the patient's interests must always come first are indicated. In the second section an argument based on the sophisticated utilitarianism of Hare (1981) is offered to show that health economics based on welfare maximization is entirely compatible with acceptance that doctors owe their patients a special (but not absolutely overriding) moral obligation to benefit them, greater than any obligations they have to benefit people in general.

9.1. Two simplistic stereotypes

There is a stereotype of medical ethics according to which the overriding moral obligation of doctors is to their individual patients such that when other moral considerations, including a concern for justice, conflict with that overriding obligation to the individual patient, concern for the patient must *always* take precedence.

There is another stereotype of the ethics of health economics according to which the overriding moral obligation of doctors and other health care workers ought to be maximization of overall welfare, such that when a doctor's special moral concern for his or her individual patient would interfere with the achievement of a greater benefit to others then the latter must *always* take precedence over the doctor's concern for the patient.

In this paper I shall argue that these absolutist stereotypes are simplistic and that, while it is undoubtedly the case that doctors do and ought to have

114

a special moral concern for their patients, they also both ought to have, and do in fact in their practice acknowledge themselves to have, other medico-moral concerns which may override this special concern for any particular patient. These competing moral concerns include a concern for justice, in the sense of fair allocation among competing claims, and this concern may and does sometimes express itself in monetary terms. I shall illustrate the empirical aspect of these claims mainly from my own field of general practice (primary care) but also from more general considerations of medical practice. In addition I shall argue that even from the utilitarian starting point of many health economists there is good reason to uphold the traditional special moral concern for their patients which doctors individually and professionally impose upon themselves. Thus there need not be and should not be any unbridgeable moral chasm between medical ethics and health care economics.

9.2. 'The individual patient's interests alwasy come before social considerations'

The first simplistic stereotype—which argues for the moral supremacy of concern for the individual patient—is undoubtedly held by some members of the medical profession, at least when they are arguing theoretically. Levinsky probably writes for many doctors in stating: 'physicians are required to do everything that they believe may benefit each patient without regard to costs or other societal considerations. In caring for an individual patient the doctor must act solely as that patient's advocate, against the apparent interests of society as a whole, if necessary' (Levinsky 1984).

Kemperman writes that 'the sole duty of the curative doctor is to help his patients, and that he has no wider responsibility' (Kemperman 1982). He adds, however, that there is a separate role for 'public (or political) medicine' which involves the laying down of the conditions under which the curative doctor works and under which considerations of welfare maximization or the overall minimization of suffering may be appropriate. The chairman of the British Medical Association's Central Ethical Committee, Dr Sandy Macara, is reported to have said that considerations of triage in order to make best use of inadequate resources must never be applied to care of the terminally ill. Triage might be appropriate on the battlefield but it should not be extended to care of the dying. 'What worries me is that some people seem to be dragging in the question of the terminally ill and saying that if resources are rationed we have to make the best use of them . . . While it might often be appropriate to avoid heroic surgery, for example, this must always be because it is not worth it to the patient, never because of pressure on resources' (Edwards 1983).

Conflicting interests of different patients

Now few people would fail to sympathize with the moral objective behind these statements—the best possible medical care of the individual patient—and few would fail to wish it were possible to attain it. However, the moral dilemma arises when, for one reason or another, if that objective is to be met, then some other moral value is threatened: in that context the notion that the doctor's duty to the individual patient must always take precedence seems counter-intuitive in theory (it seems unjust or unfair) and it also seems inaccurate as an account of how doctors in practice behave. Thus in practice most doctors recognize moral obligations to *all* their patients, and do not accept that the index patient's interests must always come first (the index patient being the one whom the doctor is at the time attending). For example suppose I as a general practitioner am seeing a patient with severe psychological problems and am listening to an intimate and delicate account of his personal anguish. Suddenly my phone goes—a 55-year-old patient with chest pain has collapsed in the waiting room. I'm the only doctor available. I, like almost any colleague I know, would leave my index patient in order that I could attend to the one outside. But of course that is to subordinate the interests of my patient of the moment (the index patient) to the interests of the patient outside. The reason I, and I presume most doctors who behaved similarly, would offer in justification is that at that moment I perceived myself to have a greater obligation to the patient who might be having a heart attack outside than to my index patient with his psychological problems.

The interests of patients as a group versus the interests of others

But, it might be protested, that is nothing to do with the point at issue, which concerns a conflict between the doctor's obligation to his or her patients on the one hand and the requirements of society on the other. Note first the slide in this counter-argument away from the original claim—that it is the index patient (singular) who takes moral priority, to the fall-back claim that it is a doctor's patients (plural) who collectively take priority. As soon as we agree that we may have to give up, at least for the time being, our efforts for one of our patients in the interests of another whose needs we consider more pressing, we have done two things: we have implicitly rejected the original claim that our moral concern for the patient of the moment always takes precedence, and we have begun to rely on some sort of assessment of where our moral priorities lie when there are conflicting demands made upon our (personal) medical resources: in other words we have begun to rely on *some* principle of justice, however rudimentary and inchoate. In this case the implicit criterion relied on might be that immediately life-threatening conditions take moral precedence over psychological problems. Such a criterion is, I would in other contexts argue, neither necessary nor sufficient for an adequate theory of justice in the allocation of medical resources—but that is another matter. The point of the example is simply to indicate both the moral implausibility of always giving priority to the interests of the index patient and the unlikelihood of doctors in practice actually doing so.

How in practice the interests of others sometimes supersede the interests of patients

So what about the fall-back position—that a doctor's moral obligations to his or her *patients* (plural) always take precedence over the interests of others? Again this seems intuitively somewhat implausible, and when clinical examples are adduced even more implausible, as an absolute principle. Perhaps the strongest counter-examples to offer health care professionals come from consideration of three groups of people in the context of what is likely actually to happen in clinical practice. The first is the class of people who are sick but are not any doctor's patients. Presumably a large proportion of the sick people in the world come into that category, but, even if we limit our consideration to the sick of the developed world there are still many sick people who do not happen to be any doctor's patients. Now I do not for one moment believe that we as a profession take enough moral concern for the sick who are not our patients—but in this context all I need to show is that in practice we *sometimes* believe we ought to place the interests of those who are not our patients before those of our patients. And, just as many GPs would rush out of their consultation to do what they could for the patient in the waiting room who had collapsed with chest pain, so too they would probably do the same if the person was a total stranger who had collapsed outside in the street and they were called. Another less obvious example arises whenever a GP takes a new patient on to his or her list who is not currently a patient of any other doctor; for by adding to the list size the doctor is in fact reducing the time and resources available to the existing patients. While this may not amount to very much difference in the case of a single additional patient, presumably the amount of time a doctor with a list of 1500 patients has to give to each patient is considerably more than the amount of time the same doctor would have to give with a list of 2500 patients (assuming, implausibly, but for the purpose of the argument that other commitments are the same in both cases). This is not a criticism of such action, but simply points out that in practice doctors do sometimes give priority to the medical interests of people who are not (yet) patients at the expense of the interests of their existing patients (the fact that self-interest plays a part in such decisions does not negate the point!).

Second, consider the interests of future patients. Quite a few doctors devote some of the time which they would otherwise be giving to their current patients to carrying out medical research. Much of this research is not intended to benefit their current patients but to benefit future patients—so-called non-therapeutic research. Spending time on such medical research which would otherwise be spent on current patients implies giving priority in some circumstances to the interests of future patients over the interests of current patients.

   Third, consider healthy people and the increasing interest general practitioners are taking (and being asked to take) in prevention of disease. Presumably if doctors' moral obligations to their patients must always take precedence over their obligations to others then medical efforts at prevention, which by definition are orientated to those who are currently *well*, at least in relation to what is to be prevented, can never be justified so long as the needs of currently ill patients are not entirely met—which would seem to shelve preventive medicine for the foreseeable future. Yet in practice many general practitioners spend *some* of their time on prevention. To spend time vaccinating people against diseases, indulging in health education about smoking, or diet, or exercise, or screening well patients for raised blood pressure abnormalities of the cervix, is at least sometimes to put more value on helping those who are currently healthy than on benefiting our patients. Once again this in no way criticizes such activities but simply points out that they belie the absolutist claim—even the modified one—that *our* patients' interest always come first.

Medical obligations in general versus economic considerations

Suppose, however, that by patients we mean anyone, healthy or sick, to whom we have some medical obligation, on the grounds that they are at least potentially sick. Certainly it is routine for general practitioners to talk about the number of patients on their lists meaning all the people who have 'signed on' with them for primary medical care, regardless of whether or not they are sick. Then the next fall-back argument might be that, even if the original claim is untenable (that the doctor's moral obligation to his or her patient should always take precedence over other moral concerns), and even if the first fallback claim is untenable (that doctors' obligations to their *sick* patients collectively should always take precedence over other moral claims), none the less doctors' concern for sick people (actual, potential, and future) should be morally distinguished from and take precedence over other societal concerns, especially economic concerns, when these conflict with the medical obligation to alleviate the plight of the (actual, potential, and future) sick. While others in society can and should legitimately concern themselves with these other societal and especially economic concerns, doctors should not, their role should be to do the best they can for the sick, in this extended sense. The trouble is that 'the sick' in this extended sense includes everyone: for many, perhaps most of us, are in the class of 'future sick', and *all* of us are in the class of potentially sick. Thus the broad reformulation of the original principle that 'the patient's interests always come first' required by the counter-examples offered requires *everybody's* interests to come first!

Ah, but not their *economic* interests, it might be protested, only their *health* interests. Well the first response to that is that economic interests can be *any* interests that contribute to people's overall benefits and overall harms, including health and illness. Economists, contrary to popular belief, are not just interested in money (Drummond and Mooney 1983). Thus *any* interests doctors consider they ought to take into account when deciding how to treat people *are*, as I understand it, at least potentially 'economic interests'. However, what people generally mean by 'economic interests' is 'monetary' or 'financial' interests. Is the claim that monetary interests ought always to be excluded from medical consideration and decision making tenable? Once again I think the answer is no. Surely it is obvious that sometimes at least the cost to others of some potentially beneficial medical intervention will simply be too great to be justified, and I believe that the following examples will demonstrate that in practice doctors do not behave as if monetary considerations should *never* be considered.

Exercise ECGs, cervical cytology, and costs

As I said earlier, general practitioners are increasingly asked to take on responsibilities for prevention. But the cost of prevention can be very high. To take one example, there can be little doubt that an annual full medical examination with a wide range of screening tests would be beneficial to at least a small percentage of all who undertook to be thus examined. There can equally be little doubt that, among the various diagnostic tests, an exercise ECG in men over the age of 45 would be diagnostically more efficient than a static ECG (which would at present be part of the normal screening process in such people). If the purpose of such screening is to detect the earliest signs of heart disease so as to take preventive measures in those who have them, then it seems sensible to do the more accurate exercise ECG rather than the standard static ECG. But where is the money to come from, and at what cost to other possible uses? The fact is that in British general practice exercise ECGs are not requested as part of routine medicals, and if one asked GPs why not they would almost certainly say that the cost to the National Health Service of requesting such screening would be too great in comparison to the benefits to the small proportion of people who would benefit by such screening. (They are also aware of the fact that even if they requested exercise ECGs as part of such screening they would not get them. The rationing would be carried out by the doctors in charge of the cardiology departments responsible for carrying out the exercise ECGs, and again if those doctors were asked why they would presumably give excessive cost as the justification.)

Now exercise ECGs are not of widespread interest (yet) but a similar problem of resource allocation in general practice is much more widely recognized to exist with cervical screening. A test exists whereby cells can be scraped from the surface of the cervix of the uterus and sent to a cytology laboratory for microscopical examination. Not only can cancer of the cervix be detected by this method before the stage at which it produces clinical symptoms, but also some of the potentially precursor conditions which are not themselves cancer but which are known to be more likely to be followed by cancer if they are left untreated. What is the 'correct' frequency for screening for such disorders? From the individual woman's point of view it is probably true to assert that the more frequently she has a cervical smear the less likely she is to die of cancer of the cervix. At any rate from the individual woman's point of view annual smears might well be a reasonable minimum, and if she could be bothered to have the test every 3 months she would probably decrease her chances yet further of allowing the rare but more rapidly fatal forms of cervical cancer to develop beyond the state at which they are likely to be curable. Of course the probability that halving the interval between tests will be of benefit becomes progressively and asymptotically smaller with each such reduction of interval. None the less *some* increased probability of benefit, however minute, can be expected in proportion to the frequency with which such screening tests are performed.

Similar sorts of reasoning can be applied to the expensive form of breast X-ray known as mammography, which detects breast cancer at an early stage, well before it can be reliably detected by simply feeling the breast. If the woman's own interests were the only ones to be considered then cervical screening and mammography should be provided routinely on the National Health Service at whatever frequency the individual woman wishes, and from the point of view of the general practitioner there could be no justification for refusing such requests. Yet at the time of writing there is no national provision of mammography under the NHS, though some NHS hospitals do provide it for screening purposes, and so far as cervical screening is concerned the UK health departments recommend doing the test every 5 years in women under the age of 35, while local cytology departments offer their own guidelines on the frequency with which they are prepared and able to carry out microscopical examination of cervical smears. Even if the laboratory facilities were freely available on the National Health Service there can be very few general practitioners who would be prepared to carry out the smears themselves as frequently as the individual woman might wish (suppose a woman wanted one every day) even though it is clear that the risk to the individual woman would be progressively reduced the more often she had these tests. Part of such reluctance on the part of the GP would of course be self-interest—but a significant part would surely be that to carry out the tests so frequently would put unreasonable financial burdens on the National Health Service and thus the taxpayer.

Comprehensive medical screening

These examples can be extended. Indeed there seems no doubt that a comprehensive medical screening service for the nation's entire population, provided as often as individuals wanted to be screened, would benefit *some* of the people thus screened. If every GP provided such a service to all the people on his or her NHS list who wanted it there is no doubt that *some* of them would benefit. But such provision would be an overwhelming burden on the GP's resources (from whom should the extra time such screening required be taken and why?), upon the secondary diagnostic resources of the National Health Service, such as pathology laboratories, radiology departments, and ECG departments, and upon the taxpayer. Thus the idea that doctors in general and GPs in particular act on the assumption that they should never be concerned with financial considerations is not borne out in practice. (It is of course another matter *how much* they take financial considerations into account, how much they *should* do so, and how much their criteria should be explicit and socially approved. Here I have only been concerned to show that in practice doctors do not follow the absolutist line that financial considerations must play no part in their medical decision making.)

A two-tier response: can clinical care be dissociated from economic considerations?

Various responses to these examples may be anticipated. One might be that in the case of screening and other activities not concerned with care of sick patients, it is reasonable to consider financial aspects, but that in the case of the care of sick patients financial considerations should always be eschewed. But once again (i) it seems obvious that *some* potential benefits to sick patients will be simply too expensive to be acceptable to third-party payers, whether these are families, nations, or contributors to insurance schemes (it is a standing joke that a trip to the Bahamas, while undoubtedly what the doctor might like to order, is not available on the National Health Service—should it be?); and (ii) if we look at what doctors in practice actually do we see that even in patient care doctors do sometimes take financial considerations into account.

A variant of this response is to try to divide up the medical role so that at the very least, as it is often argued, (by Kemperman, as above, and in this symposium explicitly by Ten Have in Chapter 3 and perhaps, implicitly, even by Mooney and McGuire in Chapter 2) a two-level approach is required whereby doctors when dealing with their patients, and especially when dealing with them in their role as curative or therapeutic doctors, must not consider questions of finance or indeed of resource allocation. On the other hand, according to this response, doctors *do* have a morally legitimate contributory role at the level of allocating the health care resources that curative doctors (including perhaps themselves) are to have · at their disposal. While a rough and ready distinction of this sort may be appropriate, it is important to realize that, even at the therapeutic/curative level of medical practice, micro-allocation decisions which involve financial considerations are frequently likely both to be morally relevant, and to be made in actual medical practice. Common to both these responses is the claim that in their therapeutic role doctors should never take economic considerations into account in their decision making. Once again it seems clear both that such a policy would be undesirable and that in practice doctors do not operate it—that is, in practice they do sometimes let financial considerations override the interests of the patient. Perhaps an admittedly dramatic example will illustrate both claims.

A clinical counter-example

I recall a patient who bled massively from his inoperable cancer of the stomach. I was the houseman and I had a strong sense that I must do my utmost for my patient; I ordered large quantitites of blood to be cross-matched and set up an infusion to replace the blood the patient had lost. It was not that I believed the blood would *cure* him, but it would very probably save his life for a while longer, whereas without the blood transfusion he would probably have died there and then. A few days later the patient had another massive bleed and I again ordered more blood and set up a transfusion. Again the patient survived what would amost certainly have been a fatal blood loss. The patient himself, knowing his situation, was keen to 'fight it, as hard as possible'. After the second massive bleed and equally massive blood transfusion my chief gently pointed out that there was no point in pouring in the blood as I had been—the patient had widespread cancer secondaries, his stomach was riddled with cancer and likely to bleed whenever the cancer eroded a blood vessel; blood trans-fusions could do no more than prolong the patient's life by a very short time. If I went on ordering blood at the prodigious rate I had been I would literally break the bank—the blood bank—causing enormous expense while seriously jeopardizing the chances of other patients for whom a blood transfusion could really be life saving rather than merely death prolonging. (What it might be asked is the morally significant difference?) I wanted to discuss all this with the patient—but he died the same day from a further massive bleed—and that time I simply was not called. My superior had decided that there was nothing beneficial that could be done. More precisely, however, his analysis was surely based on a different assessment, notably that the benefit to the patient of repeated blood transfusions each time his stomach cancer bled, even if he himself wanted to fight to the last second, was insufficient to justify the enormous cost (to others) of providing the blood.

Of course it might be argued that cost to others did not come into the assessment and that it was only the patient's own best interests which decided the matter. However, (i) I know as a matter of fact that it *was* cost which decided the matter—and the main point of this example is to show that in practice doctors do not always exclude third-party cost considerations when these conflict with their therapeutic obligations to their individual parients. Further (ii) those who would wish to argue that it *was* in the patient's best medical interests not to have been given blood and to have been allowed to die, despite his desire to fight to the last (thus evading the conclusion from this case that sometimes financial considerations do in practice override the therapeutic interests of the patient) might be more persuaded by a hypothetical variant of the case. Suppose I had had a chance to discuss these economic considerations with the patient and suppose he had continued to say that he wanted to fight to the last possible moment, with blood transfusions each time he bled, until eventually he died despite the blood transfusions. Suppose he had said that his main concern was to fight death as long as he possibly could, and that even if he only gained a few days or even a few hours, let alone a few weeks, this would be worth while as far as he was concerned. Should his assessment have prevailed or should further transfusions have been withheld? If financial considerations were barred, presumably the patient should have been given blood transfusions for as long as he wanted such treatment. Indeed, to generalize, presumably if the premiss is accepted that third-party financial considerations must never be allowed to override the doctor's therapeutic duty to his patients, then doctors should offer *any* potentially life-prolonging treatment, no matter how expensive, whenever the patient definitely and autonomously desires it. In practice this is not the way doctors actually behave. If they did those providing the finance would rapidly stop them, on the grounds (i) that they would wish to have a say in how their money is spent and (ii) that there was no obvious reason why expenditure on the sick should take priority, let alone absolute priority, over all sorts of other potential benefits which would otherwise have to be forgone.

Does rationing 'in the patient's best interests' evade the economic dilemma?

Here a further counter-argument can be anticipated, especially from certain quarters in my own profession. According to this counter-argument patients should not necessarily be given the medical treatments and resources they *want*, even if they do have some likelihood of prolonging their lives. It is up to the doctor to decide whether or not such treatments and resources would really benefit them, not on grounds of third-party costs or on any grounds that considered adverse effects on others, but entirely on the basis of the patient's own good. Doctors would then have a rationing role, but their rationing would be based entirely on their assessment of how beneficial the medical resource would actually be to the patient concerned. I have argued elsewhere about the moral inadequacies of medical paternalism as a general medico-moral working principle (Gillon 1986) but here the point is simpler. Suppose the treatment in question cost nothing, or very little (say the cost of a cheap meal), the patient (autonomously) wanted it, and there was *some* prospect, however small, of benefit to the patient. Suppose for example there was about a 10 per cent probability that a medical treatment which cost the same as a hospital dinner would prolong a patient's life by an additional day or two, and the patient wanted the treatment. More specifically suppose the blood that I was pouring into my patient all those years ago only cost a penny or two a pint and was widely available. How many doctors would argue that they should withhold even *cheap* potentially life-saving or indeed merely death-prolonging treatments because they believed, contrary to the patient's belief, that it would not significantly benefit the patient? Very few, I suspect.

Similarly, suppose the treatment was reasonably widely available but extremely expensive (say it was based on platinum or gold) and the patient wealthy and willing to pay for it. How many doctors would deny the treatment then? Again very few I suspect. Yet if the counter-argument we are considering is accepted (that the doctor should impose his view of what is in the patient's interests over the patient's own view) then doctors *should* refuse such treatments. The fact, if I am right in thinking that it is a fact, that few would deny such treatments provided either that they were cheap, or that the patient paid for them, shows that in practice it is the cost to others which determines their decision, at least in part. To avoid any danger of self-deception on this point it would be worth while for any doctor who wishes to withhold a treatment 'in the patient's best interests' but against the patient's autonomous wishes to ask himself whether he would withhold it if the patient were quite happy to pay the entire cost, or if the treatment were very cheap and easily available. If in those circumstances the doctor would be prepared to provide the treatment or other medical resource then clearly his original decision must have been based at least in part on consideration of third-party costs.

It was argued during discussion of this paper at the conference to which it was given that in some cultures doctors do indeed withhold life-saving resources even when the patient wants them and is willing to pay for their entire costs. Thus according to Professor Uhde, a Norwegian economist, if in Norway a patient was not selected for the state-provided renal dialysis programme it would be *illegal* for the patient to buy such care privately, and for doctors to provide it. While vigorous discussion ensued about the moral justification of such a law, the example is not a counter-example to this particular claim, which is that doctors would in general not be prepared *simply on the grounds of their assessment of the patient's best interests* to stop a patient paying for life-saving resources which he or she autonomously desired. The example, offered by Professor Uhde merely shows that in some cultures doctors go considerably further than I have been indicating (and would be prepared to justify) in allowing other considerations—here presumably a particular concept of justice—to override the principle that the patient's interests always come first.

Examples can be multiplied indefinitely in the context of hospital practice of the potentially enormous cost of increasingly expensive medical techniques for prolonging life—respirators of one sort or another, dialysis, artificial nutrition, an incredible variety of surgical operations, acute resuscitation procedures at the time of cardiac and/or pulmonary arrest, and a wide range of chemical, surgical, and radiotherapeutic techniques with which to try to defeat cancer. And what about the totally implantable (and totally expensive) artificial heart when that is finally developed? If the actual and reasonably anticipated behaviour of doctors responsible for such life-saving techniques were relentlessly investigated I have little doubt that it could be demonstrated unequivocally that in practice hospital doctors *do* sometimes allow cost to others to override benefit to the patient.

Economic considerations in drug prescribing
Similar problems and similar responses also arise, if less dramatically, in general practice. I recall a woman with arthritis who came to ask for the latest and most expensive non-steroidal anti-inflammatory drug (NSAID) on the advice of the private doctor she had seen. We are not supposed to prescribe National Health Service drugs on behalf of private doctors but she was also a National Health Service patient of ours and obviously I had to assess and treat her arthritis appropriately. It turned out that she had not even tried the ordinary and far cheaper anti-inflammatories and I suggested that she start with aspirin, a highly effective very cheap NSAID with probably no worse a record of side-effects than the other more expensive drugs. If she really wanted to start with one of the most expensive drugs on the market I had no doubt that her private specialist would be perfectly happy to issue her a private prescription. She was outraged. She wanted 'the best', and in particular she wanted what the specialist had recom-

mended, and she could not see why she should not be given it on the National Health Service rather than having to pay the very high market price. She transferred to another doctor. Now if I had *not* been acting to some degree as custodian of the public purse I should not have denied her the more expensive drug she wanted. Under the split role strategy we are considering and in my role as a 'curative' doctor I should presumably have had no concern for the economic aspects of the matter and given her the drug she wanted and which she had faith in. But I think that I am not exceptional in the ranks of general practitioners in denying her that NHS prescription on the grounds of unjustified cost. (I had no way of telling at the time that the drug she requested was subsequently to be taken off the market because of the higher than average incidence of fatal side-effects.)

Another common example in general practice of cost considerations conflicting with the best interests of the patient arises in the treatment of acne. Oxytetracycline is in the large majority of cases an effective and very cheap treatment. However, it is probable that a different form of tetra-cycline, minocycline, is both somewhat more effective and slightly less likely to produce nasty side effects than oxytetracycline, though in both cases nasty side-effects are very rare. Yet I, like many other general practitioners, in practice normally start with oxytetracycline and only switch to the more expensive drug if the oxytetracycline is not sufficiently effective. This is entirely on grounds of cost to the NHS (and thus to the taxpayer). Are we wrong and should we routinely prescribe the more expensive drug as drug of first choice? To me it seems a reasonable balance between my special obligation to my patients and my obligations to society. Yet there is no doubt that if economic considerations are not to affect me in my role as a 'curative doctor' I should in general start with the more expensive drug because it is somewhat more likely to be effective than is the cheaper one and perhaps even less likely to have nasty side-effects (though I emphasise that in both cases such side-effects are extremely unlikely). In any case, as far as the empirical claim is concerned, the fact that I and many other GPs tend to start with the cheaper oxytetracycline once again shows that in practice doctors do sometimes place cost to the NHS (and thus to the taxpayer) above the patient's interests.

Microbiological throat swabs for every sore throat?

A further set of economic concerns in practice limits the use by NHS general practitioners of diagnostic resources, in terms of both diagnostic tests and referral for specialist assessment. If money were no object one might do many more standard investigations than we do at present. Take one example: the throat swab. Normally when someone comes with a sore throat we say wait for the first 4 or 5 days because the vast majority of such infections are caused by viruses for which we have no cure, and in any case most of them get better within that time thanks to the body's own defences. If after 4 or 5 days the sore throat is not improving then we usually give the person some penicillin on the grounds that bacterial infection, whether primary or secondary, is likely to have occurred. Should we, however, take throat swabs and test for bacteria, mycoplasmas, and viruses routinely in cases of sore throats? 'Of course not' would be the standard general practitioner's response (not to mention the standard bacteriologist's) on the grounds that the chances of such surveillance benefiting any patient would be extremely small, whereas the cost would be extremely great.

None the less if I had routinely done such screening on everyone with a sore throat I would possibly have averted appalling consequences for one of our patients. He had a throat infection caused by a mycoplasma. The mycoplasma got into his bloodstream, lodged in blood vessels in his spinal cord, produced a miniature thrombosis which blocked off the local blood-supply and thus caused him to be permanently paralysed from the waist down. Now if I had routinely looked for mycoplasma in all people with sore throats when they first appeared in the surgery that patient might well have been treated with the appropriate antibiotic and never have had his rarest of rare complications. (There have probably only been a half dozen cases ever reported of mycoplasma transverse myelitis.) But the cost implications of routine investigations for mycoplasma in every person with a sore throat are enormous.

The cost of the sixth stool guaiac test

Drummond and Mooney (1983) refer to a similar sort of concern pursued by Neuhauser and Lewicki (1975) who assessed the costs of doing consecutive stool guaiac tests to detect cancer of the bowel. Each test detected existing but silent bowel cancers in 92 per cent of cases. If six rounds of such tests were done the average overall cost for detecting a case of bowel cancer was less than $2500. However the cost of detecting such a cancer by use of the sixth consecutive stool test was $47m per case detected. Although I have not done the calculation for prevention of mycoplasma transverse myelitis by the use of routine throat swabs for sore throats I should be surprised if the cost would not be many millions of pounds per case prevented. *Should* we spend very large sums of money on investigations which will only prove beneficial in a tiny proportion of people? Although the probability of averting harm may be very low and the cost very high, the fact remains that for many such medical risks the harmful effects when they do occur may be horrendous for the affected person. What sorts of probabilities of what sorts of harms justify what sorts of expenditures? Or are we as curative doctors really to exclude all consideration of cost to others? Although I have not done any formal surveys I am quite sure that the majority of British general practitioners do not accept that absolutist line in their everyday practice, and examples of some sort of rough and ready cost benefit analysis can be extracted from almost all investigations one decides to do or not to do in general practice. When one knows that a National Health Service with limited diagnostic resources is to carry out the investigations one orders there is in practice always at the back of one's mind, as part of the overall cost–benefit assessment (however crude this may be) not *only* the cost and benefit to the patient but also the cost to the National Health Service (and thus to the community which funds it). If one were to take thoroughly to heart the idea that as curative doctors we should *never* allow concern for cost to others to deflect us from doing whatever we could to benefit our patients, then diagnostic services would be overwhelmed as we tested for rare but possible problems for which some beneficial measures were available, if only the problem were discovered.

I am not arguing of course that this role as custodian of the national purse *benefits* our patients. On the contrary my point is that a small proportion of them may be seriously harmed as a result, as perhaps was our unfortunate patient who developed a mycoplasma transverse myelitis from his sore throat. On the other hand if we were not to consider third-party costs at all—if as curative doctors we were only to consider the best possible interests of our patients—then the resource implications to the National Health Service would be enormous, and I hope that I have demonstrated that in practice doctors do not behave according to such absolutist principles. I also hope that I have at least suggested that it would be very worrying for us au a community if they did! However, as Professor Mooney said at the conference to which this paper was presented, if we as doctors *are* to be basing even our clinicial judgements to some extent on economic considerations, then perhaps we should do so explicitly, where possible in ways that take the best available cost and benefit data into consideration, and using criteria approved in some way by the community in which we practise.

Recapitulation

So far then I have argued that despite the theoretical claims of some doctors that 'the patient's interests must always come first' most doctors as a matter of fact do in their everyday practice believe they ought in some circumstances to allow the interests of others—including the economic interests of others—to take precedence over the best interests of a particular patient. I have illustrated this empirical claim from practical examples drawn largely from my own specialty, general practice, showing how a concern for other patients for whom a doctor is responsible, for other patients of other doctors, for patients of the future (as in the case of non-therapeutic medical research), for people who are sick but not patients, and even a concern for people who are neither patients nor sick (as in the case of preventive medicine) can afford counter-examples to the claim that doctors practise according to the principle 'the patient's interests must always come first'.

Even if the claim is broadened under the pressure of such counter-examples to include the medical interests of all sick people, all future sick people, and all potentially sick people, it is still, I argued, implausible to claim that doctors do in fact always regard their interests as taking precedence over economic considerations including the costs to others of such a medical preoccupation. On the contrary, I suggested, the broader the range of such medical concern and the more economically burdensome to others it is perceived to be, the less likely doctors are, at least in general practice and probably in hospital practice too, to ignore economic considerations when they conflict with these medical interests.

I also considered the split role strategy which is sometimes offered as a way of evading the need to take economic considerations into account in medical practice. According to this position doctors are required to take account of economic considerations when they are involved with avowedly economic issues such as allocation of medical resources but are prohibited from so doing when they are in their curative or therapeutic roles. I argued that while this offered a useful rough and ready distinction, and made explicitly permissible the doctor's role in allocation of medical resources, it failed to accommodate the counter-examples that arose in ordinary patient care when economic considerations would in practice be taken into account by many doctors. And I suggested that if these economic considerations were not considered in clinical practice then totally implausible and almost certainly widely unacceptable expenditure would be required for small and/or low probability benefits to patients. It is obvious (because analytically true) that whenever doctors accept a curative role in a context of limited medical resources provided by third parties, then they *either* implicitly commit themselves to *some* form of justifiable distribution of those resources, even at the sharp end of individual curative medical care, *or* they implicitly commit themselves to having *no* justifiable basis for restricting the potentially beneficial medical resources they provide for any particular patient, no matter how small and how improbable the anticipated degree of benefit, no matter what the effect of providing such care would be on the medical care of others, and no matter what the providers of those resources would think about such use.

In practice, I have argued, doctors are indeed aware (at least in some circumstances) of the need both to use resources efficiently and with minimal waste and to ration the medical resources at their disposal in ways which balance the degree and probability of benefit for one patient against the potentially detrimental effects on others, including, at least in obvious and extreme cases, detrimental economic effects on others.

As well as arguing that in practice doctors do not take the absolutist positions sometimes claimed, and that those that did would be highly unlikely to continue to do so if they were aware of the full practical implications of such positions, I also suggested that these absolutist positions were morally unacceptable. My role in this symposium was that of a practising general practitioner with an interest in medical ethics and I leave it to others to argue the philosophical case against such absolutist concern for the patient or patients. Suffice it to assert that I know of no developed moral theory which does or plausibly could accommodate such a concern. According to any developed moral theory of which I am aware there would come a point at *some* level of economic harm to others in comparison to anticipated benefit to the patient or person concerned (discounted for probabilities in both cases) where third-party economic considerations would become morally relevant to the decision whether or not to carry out a particular investigation, treatment, or other medical intervention.

9.3.   Must doctors then be dispassionate welfare accountants?

So does this stance entail that doctors' traditional special concern for their patients, and for the sick, must be superseded by some dispassionate role as welfare accountants or hedonic calculators, always assessing possible courses of action for their possible welfare-maximizing properties and having no more concern for their patients than for anybody else? I think it is fairly clear that this is not the case even if one were to accept—as many economists and perhaps most health economists seem to accept—that the *supreme* moral objective is the utilitarian one of maximizing overall welfare (not an assumption that as a moral pluralist I do in fact share). In this next section I shall outline a *utilitarian* argument in favour of doctors' maintaining their traditional special (but not absolutely overriding) obligations to their patients.

Against simplistic utilitarianism

Those who are unaware of the subtlety and complexity of utilitarian theories, especially contemporary variants, might think it impossible for utilitarians to be able to justify such special relationships between doctors and their patients. Certainly a simplistic form of utilitarianism would be unable to do so. The philosopher G. J. Warnock (1971) puts the case against oversimple utilitarianism when he describes the fears of a patient who knows his doctor is one of these simple utilitarians. Although the patient realizes that the doctor is generally beneficent, he also realizes that the doctor does not acknowledge any special duties of beneficence towards any particular person, let alone towards any particular patient. His only moral interest is to maximize the general happiness.

Thus while he will not malevolently kill me off, I cannot be sure that he will always try to cure me of my afflictions; I can be sure only that he will do so *unless* his assessment of the 'general happiness' leads him to do otherwise . . . I could not get him to promise, in the style of the Hippocratic Oath, always and only to deploy his skills to my advantage; nor could I usefully ask him to disclose his intentions. The reason is essentially the same in each case. Though he might, if I asked him to, promise not to kill me off, he would of course keep this promise only if he judged it best on the whole to do so . . . Similarly if I ask him what his intentions are, he will answer truthfully only if he judges it best on the whole to do so . . . And this is quite general; if general felicific beneficence were the only criterion, then promising and talking alike would become wholly idle pursuits (Warnock 1971).

Against this simple version of utilitarianism, Warnock puts up a more complicated version—so-called rule utilitarianism—whereby the following of certain rules is held to be conducive to the maximizing of happiness and thus justified by utilitarianism. But he points out that the following of rules in an absolute sort of way leads to removal of judgement about the particular merits of particular cases in particular circumstances, and he suggests that in the sphere of moral judgement this is implausible (as contrasted for example with the playing of games, where rules are by convention accepted as absolute). But Warnock proceeds: if the rules are not to be seen as absolute but as themselves needing justification, which in the case of utilitarianism is presumably justification by the single and ultimate moral standard of utility, then rule utilitarianism boils down to the simple utilitarianism he has previously rejected on the grounds that one could never trust anyone to tell the truth, to keep promises, to have a special concern for one, etc. For it all depends on people's assessment of what will maximize utility in particular cases.

How sophisticated utilitarians can justify doctors' special obligations to their patients

However, sophisticated utilitarians do not, of course, have to accept that the rules according to which people should behave are *absolute* rules. If they did they would indeed be hoist by their own petards, for they would then not be permitted even in principle to override a rule when this was necessary in the interests of maximizing welfare or happiness. Various utilitarian strategies have been developed to accommodate without absolutism the intuitively important components of ordinary moral life, including such aspects as the need to be truthful, to keep one's promises, to respect people's privacy, and to maintain special relationships and special moral obligations to certain people. (See for example Smart 1973; Brandt 1979; Singer 1979; Glover 1977.)

To me the most convincing of these utilitarian strategies is that developed by Hare, a simple version of which can be found in an Institute of Medical Ethics working party report on medical research with children (Nicholson 1986). A more elaborately argued version of his thesis is also available (Hare 1981). In outline Hare argues that utilitarianism prescribes two levels of moral thinking, the intuitive and the critical. Intuitive moral thinking is the moral thinking of ordinary moral life, and includes accept- ance of (most of) the ordinary moral virtues with which we are brought up and bring up our children. Part of such ordinary moral thinking will include the need to tell the truth, keep one's promises, respect people's privacy and dignity, and so on. Also included in such intuitive moral thinking will be the notions that special obligations should be respected, including for example the special obligations of parents to their children and of doctors to their patients. In such respects utilitarian morality at the level of intuitive moral thinking will be similar to the moral thinking of ordinary moral life and of deontological pluralists (for example see Ross 1930, 1939). The big difference, according to Hare, is that while pluralists and ordinary moral thinkers stop there, and are unable to justify the various intuitive moral principles except on the grounds of notoriously unreliable appeals to intuition, utilitarianism *is* able to justify them. Thus, according to Hare, accepting these intuitive moral principles, special relationships, and unreflective virtues, is justified because, and only in so far as, doing so tends to maximize the welfare or happiness of all, considered impartially. Thus for utilitarians of Hare's ilk there must be a second tier of moral reasoning, which he calls critical thinking, which subjects ordinary or intuitive moral thinking to criticism based on the overriding moral princi- ple that the welfare of all, considered impartially, must be maximized (and he argues controversially, that this principle itself does not depend on any moral intuitions but is one that follows logically from the meaning and logical properties of certain moral words, especially 'ought').

Thus accepting the intuitive *prima facie* moral principles, developing the intuitively required dispositions to behave routinely and unreflectively in ways that conform to such principles, and ensuring that such norms are maintained throughout society—all these can be entirely compatible with utilitarianism. At the same time they can manifest the sort of respect for individual people, the respect for doing one's duty and following 'the moral law', which deontological thinkers including Kant extol. Included amongst such intuitively desirable dispositions are dispositions for parents to have special and partial (as distinct from impartial) concern for their offspring and for doctors to have special and partial concern for their patients. But critical thinking which favours such departures from impartiality 'is itself impartial; it favours them because their inculcation will be for the best for all considered impartially' (Hare 1981, p. 129).

Economics can be concerned with process as well as outcome

Thus it is perfectly possible for utilitarianism—which as I have indicated seems to be the favoured moral philosophical stance of health economists—to justify the claim that doctors *should* have and should continue to have a special relationship with, and special obligations to, their patients. This should be a partial as distinct from an impartial relationship that requires more concern than each of us owes to other people in general. To put it into the economic language of Mooney and McGuire (Chapter 2), welfare maximization is not concerned merely with outcomes; it is also concerned with the processes whereby those outcomes may be achieved. Just as Warnock *qua* patient would not like his doctor to treat him with total impartiality, as though he were just any member of the world's population, so most people when ill (at least if severely ill), and most people when thinking about what they would prefer if and when they were (severely) ill, would prefer that their doctors had a special concern for, relationship with, and obligation to, them as patients, rather than seeing them merely as interchangeable members of the population.

9.4. No unbridgeable chasm between health economics and medical ethics

On the other hand I suspect that few of us, even seeing ourselves as patients or potential patients would, once we had thought about it, want our doctors to have an *absolute* commitment to our interests such that it overrode all other commitments. Few of us, seeing ourselves as taxpayers as well as potential patients, would want doctors to feel free to spend as much of our tax-provided money as they liked on their patients, provided only that they thought there was *some* probability of benefit, no matter how small the benefit, no matter how small the probability, and no matter how great the cost. If all that empirical speculation is anywhere near accurate, and if maximization of preference satisfaction is accepted as the best way of achieving the overall moral goal of welfare maximization, then it can be seen why doctors should be exhorted to accept both a special concern for their patients *and* some responsibility to balance that concern against its various costs to others.

So far as mechanisms for balancing such potentially conflicting concerns are concerned, it would certainly seem sensible, even from a utilitarian perspective, to separate medical decision making about macro- and meso-allocation of medical resources from the sorts of clinical micro-allocation decisions which I have outlined above. But even in the clinical micro-allocation context, as I hope I have indicated, there is and always will be a need for rationing, economic efficiency, and a concern for costs, at least where health services are paid for by third parties. Such a need is already widely if not always explicitly recognized by doctors in their actual practice. There need be no untraversable gulf between sophisticated utilitarianism, including its economic variants, on the one hand and medical ethics on the other. Medical ethics in practice recognizes a variety of potentially conflicting moral objectives, and rarely are doctors willing or able to sustain a claim that any one of those principles must always take precedence over the others. Certainly an essential component of medical ethics is and should remain the special moral obligation, greater than the obligations we ordinarily owe each other, to benefit our patients. However, that special obligation does not in practice and should not in theory override all our other moral obligations, including a general obligation to act justly or fairly.

References

Brandt, R. B. (1979). *A theory of the good and the right*. Oxford University Press, Oxford.

Drummond, M. and Mooney, G. (1983). *Essentials of health economics*. Northern Health Economics, University of Aberdeen, Aberdeen.

Edwards, S. (1983). No room for triage in NHS. *Medical News*, 15/22 December p. 27.

Gillon, R. (1986). Autonomy and consent. In Lockwood, M. (ed.) *Moral dilemmas in modern medicine*. Oxford University Press, Oxford.

Glover, J. (1977). *Causing death and saving lives*. Penguin, Harmondsworth.

Hare, R. M. (1981). *Moral thinking*. Oxford University Press, Oxford.

Kemperman, C. J. F. (1982). Clinical decisions. *Lancet* ii, 1222.

Levinsky, N. G. (1984). The doctor's master. *New England Journal of Medicine* 311, 1573–5.

Neuhauser, D. and Lewicki, A. M. (1975). What do we gain from the sixth stool guaiac? *New England Journal of Medicine* 293, 226–8.

Nicholson, R. H. (ed.) (1986). *Medical research with children: ethics law and practice*. Oxford University Press, Oxford. See the chapter entitled 'The structure of the argument'.

Ross, W. D. (1930). *The right and the good*. Oxford University Press, Oxford.

Ross. W. D. (1939). *Foundations of ethics*. Oxford University Press, Oxford.

Singer, P. (1979). *Practical ethics*. Cambridge University Press, Cambridge.

Smart, J. J. C. (1973). An outline of a system of utilitarian ethics. In Smart, J. C. C. and Williams, B. (eds.) *Utilitarianism for and against*. Cambridge University Press, Cambridge.

Warnock, G. J. (1971). *The object of morality*. Methuen, London.

10
Medical ethics and economics in medical education—why and how?

JOHANNES VANG

Summary

Recently there has been a growing feeling that it is important to society at large, and to health care in particular, that more emphasis is put on philosophical analysis of current problems, and that education in philosophy of science and ethics is regarded as indispensable in the teaching of medicine, nursing, and health care administration.

Key influences contributing to this view emanate from the changing social and economic environment in which health services are offered and the changing relationship and interaction between physician and patient. The problems surrounding the right to health care, distributive justice, and the allocation of resources probably constitute the strongest incentive to the present encouragement and introduction of new academic intersectoral fields, such as health economics, technology assessment, health service research, and to the rising demand for education of physicians in ethics and health economics.

It is argued that the teaching of ethics and the principles of health economics must be part of medical education.

As to the question: Who should teach it, faculty of philosophy or humanities or medicine? there may be no single answer, but it is the author's opinion that the responsibility ought to rest with the faculty of medicine, which would then collaborate intensively with the other relevant faculties.

Although concern about ethics and moral rules runs as a 'red thread' through the practice of medicine, the systematic teaching of ethics in medical schools has not been customary. The reason for this may be that medical ethics has often been confused with rules of proper professional conduct rather than being understood as the branch of philosophy which studies the rational process for deciding the best action when facing conflicting choices. Often, therefore, the only formal ethical instruction received by medical students has been on their graduation day, when they have been requested to recite 'codes of ethics' or sets of 'ethical rules' aimed at protecting patients and strengthening professional cohesion, often based on the Hippocratic Oath to add a touch of history, pomp, and magnificence to the occasion.

Recently, however, there has been a growing feeling that it is important to society at large, and to health care in particular, that more emphasis is put on philosophical analysis of current problems, and that education in philosophy of science and ethics is regarded as indispensable in the teaching of medicine, nursing, and health care administration. Several factors have contributed to this view. Some of these are well known to the public through discussions in the media and are related to the development of new technologies based on new biological knowledge. Examples are: genetic engineering, reproductional control, test-tube babies, behavioural control, the question of heart transplantation and death criteria, and the distressing extension of life of the hopelessly ill through intensive, high-technological care as presently exemplified by the artificial heart.

Other factors are presented to the public in a less conspicuous way, but are matters of doubt and discussion among health care professionals. Among these are some screening procedures, the introduction of some new and costly diagnostic procedures with no or marginal effect on health outcome, and some activities in the field of oncology.

10.1. Health policy decisions and ethics

Many of the key influences, however, emanate from the changing social and economic environment in which health services are offered. The relationship and interaction between physician and patient have been modified by the change of 'contract', as described by McGuire and Mooney (Chapter 2), partly through cost sharing by the patient with a third-party payer and partly through responsibility sharing by the physician not only with other physicians, called in for a second or third opinion or colleagues in a working collective as in a hospital setting, but also and perhaps more important by sharing the responsibility with the public and the patient. This has happened partly through a better general education of the public, but also through better information given to the individual patient, informed consent traditions, the introduction of care programmes and consensus conferences with public participation and, not least, through an increasingly improved informing of the public through the media. The patient has often been characterized as an uninformed customer, an ignorant, helpless buyer of services, the value of which he is unable to judge. This may still be true in some instances but much less so than a couple of decades ago, at least in the developed countries.

The concept of health care as a 'right' and not a 'privilege' of the wealthy, as advanced by the modern welfare state, has also introduced into health care polcy the idea of distributive justice and the issue of allocation of scarce resources.

In general it may be said that society as a whole, which creates the available resources, also defines the framework for individual claims on those resources. Changes in this framework can only be made through the political process which has made health care an important political issue. Yet infringements of these rules are often made by the medical profession through the introduction of new and costly methods, tacitly accepted or unrecognized by any societal control system. Society, which is caught up by its own encouragement of technological development, may adopt a lenient attitude even towards spectacular infringements, and it may fail to recognize the costly encroachment in medical practice of new standards and routines, which sometimes have little or no effect on the elimination of disease or the improvement of health.

The problems surrounding the right to health care, distributive justice, and the allocation of resources probably constitute the strongest incentive to the present encouragement and introduction of new academic inter-sectoral fields, such as health economics, technology assessment, health service research, and to the rising demand for education of physicians in ethics and health economics.

There is no need to dwell on the issue of scarce resources, except to mention that as a concept scarce resources cannot exist without a defined need. Although often spoken about, a basic need for health care does not exist—mankind has survived for a long time without such a 'need' being defined. The basic 'need' varies according to resources offered and in that sense it is not a 'need' in some absolute sense, but rather a demand. In some countries a third party may pay for some cosmetic operations, in other countries not. Is there a need for facelifts or breast reconstructions? In some instances, they will certainly improve life quality. In other countries only very basic health care is offered and expected. In other words: the health care 'need' is not a universal entity like the daily need for calories or daily fluid need. However, there is still a feeling that society has some kind of basic responsibility towards its members, and in order to grade this responsibility it may be useful to distinguish between primary, secondary, and tertiary needs. Facelifts would be a tertiary need and malaria treatment a primary one, but the categorization of all health problems would be extremely difficult. This is well illustrated by those patients who have been denied renal dialysis because of age, lack of intelligence, lifestyle etc., that is, instances where renal dialysis was not defined as a 'basic need', and consequently was not regarded as a right but as a privilege. This ethical problem has usually been solved in affluent societies by allocating more money to make dialysis a right.

When society accepts the responsibility for the cost consequences of ill health, the problem arises that the needs, as 'perceived' by the public or by individual patients, may differ from the 'real' needs, as defined by society. One may say that society redefines disease to include only those conditions of incapacity which entitle its members to economic support, that is, coverage of expenses for treatment and/or compensation for social inconveniences and income losses. When ill health is defined in this way in relation to societal 'need' definitions and norms, the physician usually acts as a 'double agent'—the society's and the patient's—in the distribution of societal benefits.

The issue of just distribution—geographically or socially—is equally complicated. As some of the more advanced welfare societies have experienced, an equal distribution of goods and power may create a 'new poverty' and a 'power-loss' feeling, for the same reasons as an equal global distribution of the total food supply might leave most people hungry but some more hungry and others less hungry than before. The distribution issue becomes a political issue where the question of expectations is a dominant force, with the media and politicians playing the leading parts.

Expectations and available resources define the 'basic need', and society's reaction through its health service system determines the pattern of allocation and costs. This procedure is influenced by many actors: the media, voters, politicians, health care professionals, interest groups, etc. Today, it is the prevailing feeling in many developed countries that society has overreacted—or to put it in economic terms—that the return on the investment in the health services in terms of improved health status of society is disappointing. The logical consequence of this is either to reduce investment or to invest differently, and, since health care decisions are made on two levels, both the quality of health policy decisions and the quality of clinical decision making have become focus points of interest.

10.2. Clinical decision making and ethics

We shall now turn to clinical decision making and its relationship to knowledge of formal ethics and health economics. First, however, we need an 'interlude' which may be useful for those readers unfamiliar with the terminology of ethics and philosophy of science. It deals very superficially with the difference between the empirical and the ethical dimension of decision making.

Interlude

Ethics is the systematic study of value concepts: 'good', 'bad', 'ought', 'right', and 'wrong'. It is a philosophical discipline and the fundamental ethics issues have been discussed and analysed for thousands of years. Medical ethics is applied ethics and is as old as medicine itself, but seems to have been rediscovered by the health professions and health economists during the last decades while struggling with the issues of patients' rights and the allocation of scarce resources.

The fundamental characteristic of an ethical problem is that there exists a real choice between different possible actions and that it is possible to place a significantly different value upon each of the possible actions or upon the consequences of the action. Thus there is a real choice as to whether one should or should not treat pneumonia in an old patient with apoplexy and a poor quality of life, and certainly different values can be put on the two options.

The answer to an ethical question is: right or wrong—good or bad; the answer to an empirical question is: true or false. The empirical question is descriptive and does not tell us which action to choose. Empirical problems can (at least in principle) be solved by experiments and observation. Ethical problems cannot be solved in this way but require that we come to terms with our values in relation to the particular question. Many physicians brought up in 'science' are uncomfortable with the fact that clinical decisions always include value judgements and continue to collect objective data even when these cannot influence the decision.

Another characteristic of an ethical statement is the 'ought' factor. The presence of this factor implies that the decision is regarded as valid for all similar circumstances. In other words ethical statements are considered universally prescriptive.

The typical ethical decision is a choice between good and evil, between better and worse, or between two mutually exclusive 'goods'. In the last case, whatever we do may be considered a 'bad' thing. This situation is well illustrated by the ethical problem which haunts the world—the allocation of scarce resources—where the use of the resources for one purpose is identical to a decision not to use the same resources for another purpose, both purposes being important but their relative importances often being difficult to judge. We shall discuss this problem separately.

Ethical statements cannot, like empirical statements, be verified or falsified by means of observation, but it would be a mistake to believe that value judgements cannot be subjected to rational discussion. Human beings living together in a community must by necessity create a moral code—a system of generally accepted values—in order to regulate their dealings with one another. This unwritten moral code must be regarded as a human construction, but in spite of that it exists independently of the individual members of the community. The moral code, which was created by previous generations, must be modified by the present generation in view of the constant changes in living conditions, but it never simply reflects the subjective preferences of the individual members of the community. An ethical statement is never true or false, but one may analyse rationally to what extent it is in agreement with a particular moral code.

It would also be wrong to adopt the relativistic view that one moral code is always as acceptable as any other. It is a minimum requirement that to the greatest possible extent a moral code is internally consistent, and it may be argued that the moral code must also reflect human nature. One may hold that the human by nature is an autonomous being and that actions which violate human autonomy are intrinsically wrong.

If medical ethics is considered in this context, it may be regarded as the application of the moral code of a particular society to problems of health care. Therefore, medical ethics is not a discipline with a common content internationally, like orthopaedics or neurology, but a culture-specific humanistic discipline. Many attempts have been made to formulate international codes of medical ethics, but it is normally found that they reflect the moral norms of particular societies. A few very basic rules of behaviour may be internationally commonly acceptable, but the validity of detailed recommendations must by necessity be restricted to a particular cultural context.

Ethical reasoning may take different forms and conflicts are inevitable. The physician who is faced with a choice between two courses of action may, for instance, ask the following three questions (Wulff 1981a):

1. Which decision has the best consequences (= the highest utility) for my patient? This approach is the mainstay of bedside medicine.
2. Which decision has the best consequences in general, if all physicians act like that under similar circumstances? The formulation differs slightly from the previous one, and the answers to the two questions may sometimes differ. The physician might, for instance, conclude that a particular, very expensive treatment is marginally better than a cheaper treatment, but that the cost would be too high if physicians always used that treatment. The general consequences would be better if this amount of money were used somewhere else in the health service. However, both these approaches have one thing in common. They are both examples of consequentialist ethics, as the physician judges the 'goodness' of different decisions by their consequences.
3. Which decision is the right one, regardless of the consequences? This approach illustrates deontological ethics (duty ethics), according to which it is believed that some actions are intrinsically wrong, whereas others are intrinsically right, notwithstanding the consequences. As an example, the physician might feel that it would be best for a cancer patient not to know the diagnosis and prognosis, but may still decide to provide this information, feeling that the patient has a right to know. Withholding it would be an example of undue paternalism and a violation of the patient's autonomy.

There is a vast amount of literature on this topic, which may be labelled medical ethics on the individual level, whereas fewer ethicists have taken an interest in medical ethics on the aggregate level. The politician or administrator in a health care system who has to define 'primary and secondary needs' and to allocate limited resources to different purposes must consider the consequences of different decisions for the population as a whole; they must reason along consequentialist lines and may be said to adopt a paternalistic attitude towards the members of society. However, their actions cannot be condemned as a violation of individual autonomy if they act in accordance with the moral code of the society which they serve, and if they have been delegated the responsibility, through a democratic process, for decision making in the health care system by the members of that society.

The foundation of the clinical decision

We shall now return to the question of clinical decision making and the traditional teaching and training of the medical profession in this respect.

It is possible to distinguish between (at least) three kinds of clinical reasoning (Wulff 1986):

1. Deductive reasoning from theoretical knowledge of the structure and functions of the human body during health and disease.
2. Inductive reasoning from past experience of 'similar' patients. Such experience can be uncontrolled or controlled.
3. Reasoning based on values.

From around the beginning of the last century, the main emphasis in teaching of medical students was on physics, chemistry, anatomy, biochemistry, physiology, pharmacology, pathology etc. From this theoretical fund of knowledge, it should be possible to deduce what would be the correct treatment in any given case. Duodenal ulcer for instance was 'caused' by too much acid in the stomach. Anticholinergics were known from human and animal experiments to reduce gastric secretion. In consequence, one could deduce that patients with duodenal ulcer ought to be treated with anticholinergics. Naturally, experience from the daily, clinical life was also important. Patients had often been seen to recover when they received this treatment, but the experience was without adequate scientific control.

In the 1960s there was a growing realization that this basis of clinical decision making was insufficient. Too many of those treatments which had been introduced on the basis of their theoretical 'rationale' turned out to be ineffective, and sometimes even harmful.

The controlled clinical trial was introduced: it was no longer considered scientifically proved that a treatment had the intended effect unless a controlled experiment had shown that this was the case. Anticholinergic treatment of peptic ulcer disease, for example, turned out not to fulfil expectations when it was subjected to controlled trials. Similar demands were made when it came to diagnostic methods. It was no longer considered sufficient to deduce that they were effective. It was necessary to collect controlled experience and provide figures for their specificity, sensitivity, false positive rate, etc. (Wulff 1981b).

However, around 1970, the framework of thinking among health professionals underwent further changes as it became clear that it was not sufficient to prove by means of controlled trials that diagnostic methods and treatments were effective. It is also important to evaluate critically if the effect in fact is desirable, or to put it in ethical terms: if the consequence of the clinical action is 'good' or 'bad'.

There is no doubt that there were often many overlapping reasons for this development. First of all, physicians in modern Western societies see more and more health problems which cannot be solved within the conventional biomedical frame of reference (which includes both deduction from theory and induction from experience). They frequently face problems such as:

1. Patients with malignant diseases who can be treated but not cured. Is it 'better' to die rapidly than to live longer with a poor quality of life?
2. Treatment of old severely handicapped patients with the prospects of a continuous poor quality of life. When is it morally justified not to treat intercurrent diseases, such as pneumonia, in such patients?
3. Treatment of alcoholics and toxicomanias. The treatment of an alcoholic consists of motivating the patient to stop drinking, but the term 'motivate' has no place within the bioscientific frame of reference. According to the scientific view, a human is a machine, not a being who acts freely from different motives.
4. Patients with 'psychosomatic' illness. How does one explain within the bioscientific frame of reference that mental phenomena may have somatic consequences? According to the biomedical model, everything is somatic.

These problems to a large extent arise from the fact that the consequences of clinical decisions are far greater than ever before. Previously, physicians were not able to prolong the life of seriously ill patients, and their actions did not have such fearful economic repercussions. It must also be remembered that the population, as a natural result of democratic development, has reacted against paternalistic medicine. People no longer accept that the physician sees himself as the expert in medical science who makes all the decisions. They demand to be respected as autonomous human beings who have the right to take an active part in the decision process.

Previously many people, especially laymen, lived under the impression that clinical medicine was an exact science and that most clinical decisions could be assessed by means of a scientific 'gold standard'. A series of studies done both in North America and in Europe, however, showed large differences in therapeutic actions towards seemingly identical diseases and these differences seemed to have no major impact on health outcome for the patients. Such variation in physicians' behaviour is to be expected if the majority of the decisions made in health care include value judgements, but it does not harmonize well with the illusion that medicine is an exact science. It is interesting that it has been possible to maintain this illusion in view of the extreme difficulties which have been faced by those who have attempted to define health and diseases, and the fuzziness of all current definitions. Nevertheless, the related realization of the importance of value judgements in clinical decision making created the environment for such diverse phenomena as malpractice suits, defensive medicine, consensus conferences, model care programmes and, of course, the development of the disciplines of health economics and technology assessment. All these considerations lead to the obvious conclusion that education in clinical decision theory, including formal education in medical ethics, is extremely important and ought to take a prominent place in medical education, both on the graduate and on the postgraduate level.

10.3. Health economics

Health economics deals with the problem of the allocation of scarce resources within health care. Therefore, it concerns both ethics, which we have considered already, and money, which has always been a sore point within health care. Already Hippocrates had strong views on the financial aspects of medical practice. Physicians have for generations regarded their patients' fees with mixed feelings and in modern socialized health care systems the issue of money between the physician and the patient has been neutralized as far as possible. The feeling that it is indecent to make money from people when they are ill (the patient being in the position of an uninformed customer with no other options than to buy) has also influenced the attitude to those industries which produce drugs or devices used in the care of patients. The size of the earnings of these industries, their marketing techniques, etc. have, rightly or wrongly, been met with substantial moral indignation by people of 'good will'. At the same time, there is a tendency to overlook the fact that these same industries produce and distribute useful drugs and devices and are responsible for a substantial part of the research which has made possible the treatment of previously lethal and disabling diseases. Still, the 'side-effects' of drug treatment are diverse in the form of overuse, and adverse reactions, costs, and medicalization of social problems and it cannot be concealed that the spin-off from selling drugs is money. That is a delicate subject.

Health economists entered the scene quite recently and have gone so far as to suggest that all the values of health care be assessed in terms of money. They suggested monetarian measures for survival and risks; they suggested monetary measures of effectiveness, benefits, and quality of life. Talking money was talking rope in a hanged man's house and they were not well received by the medical profession. Nevertheless, money is only a veil, an accounting convention, the physicial reality of which is presently slipping away into the world of electronics. The fundamental mistake that health economics is only about money to some extent clouded the import- ance of health economics for the medical profession. The role of econom- ists is to make those values more explicit which are *already* used, in other words to illuminate and make more visible not only what is actually happening but also what might happen if certain actions were taken. They attempt to make the consequences of actions explicit and thereby to improve decision making, both on the clinical and on the aggregate level. In that respect the health economist has a similar role to the statistician. He is able to point to fundamental dilemmas in the decision process by putting figures on different options and by creating models of high didactic value. The health economist is usually playing his tune on the aggregate level. On the other hand, the physician who makes decisions related to the single patient finds it difficult to accept statistical probability. For him the probability function has collapsed to a point—the likelihood function to a fact.

In validating ethical decisions physicians often like other people use a technique with deep roots in the Judaeo-Christian tradition. They usually ask: 'If I were in this patient's situation, would I like to have this done to me?' If the answer is yes, the action is then considered to be in agreement with the decision maker's set of values; that is, of course, if he has been honest, imaginative, and thoughtful. This technique, which is a quick one and useful in the busy daily work of the physician, is, however, useless in the frame of reference of the aggregate thinking public health physician or health economist. Some people, however, believe that there is a need for a development away from an egocentric moral, that man has to learn, that his own ego has no metaphysical or in other ways privileged position as compared with other egos, and if he steps outside his own ego and watches it as one among others, then he will have to conclude: 'I have to be treated the same way as others'. This reasoning does, however, lead to a moral which is not yet accepted, not even in theory. This view *in extremis* would mean that the moral obligation is never to make one person privileged at somebody else's expense.

Such ethics would as a consequence maintain that human values such as love and friendship become immoral. It would be wrong to give more emphasis to a close and loved one's suffering than to the anonymous suffering around the world. Such a morality is not only unrealistic but cannot be asked of the physician, who then at the same time is asked to establish an empathic and compassionate relationship with his patient, but still to see him and his suffering as an equal part of an aggregate suffering. This problem represents a significant obstacle in the training of the physician for societal responsibility for his actions.

The above reasoning, however, does not make teaching of health economics or. discussion of the ethical issue of scarce resources less important. On the contrary, visualizing and making explicit the values used in decision making under uncertainty would seem, all other things equal, to improve decisions relative to the prevailing moral laws. It is also worth considering the different roles of physicians throughout their careers. Many physicians act not only as clinical decision makers and their patients' agents, and, as we have seen previously, as agents for society, but also as department heads or as advisers to policy makers or health care politicians. In these last respects, a more intimate knowledge of the problems at the aggregate level and of health economics is a necessity. Teaching of health economics, therefore, may not only have a place in the graduate curriculum, but may be even more important in postgraduate education.

10.4.   How should education in ethics and health economics be organized?

In 1980 the Council for International Organizations of Medical Sciences (CIOMS) hosted a round-table conference on medical ethics and medical education in Mexico City. The proceedings of that conference were published by the Council for International Organizations in 1981. Recently the World Health Organization, European Office, has issued an overview of the teaching of health economics in Europe. From these publications it can be deduced that ethics is taught by most and health economics by many universities, but with considerable variation in different countries.

Since the mid 1960s ethics has been taught at most North American medical schools, more than two-thirds of the South American Schools and the majority of European medical schools. In some countries of Catholic Christian denomination, ethics is still part of the complex of legal medicine and deontology. Obviously big variations in the approach to such education will be found in these thousands of schools, from a few lecturers in medical etiquette to continuous courses of medical ethics and humanity integrated into the preclinical and clinical curriculum, including teaching in health economics and technology assessment.

The author is not aware of any studies that show if such teaching has improved health care, but there are some surveys indicating a raised awareness and understanding of ethical issues and value questions in health care by students who have attended such courses. None of these, however, indicates whether any method of teaching is superior to others.

Teaching of ethics (including the ethics of animal experimentation) and the principles of health economics must be part of medical education. The term 'bioethics' is sometimes used to describe ethical problems that arise in biology and medicine and might have been a useful term in this context, had it not been that it has already been used to describe a specific unifying theory for the interaction between science and ethics proposed by Potter. So to avoid confusion we shall discuss education in medical ethics as a part of education in medical decision making in its widest sense, and we shall consider health economics like biostatistics as a subentity within that framework.

It has been questioned whether the medical student in the preclinical years is mature enough to benefit from education in ethics. This view may be related more to the nature of traditional teaching of philosophy and ethics than to the age and level of experience of the student. It is, in fact, possible to discuss ethical issues with 11-year-old children, who also make value judgements daily, if the issues are discussed at their level of experience. The frame of reference created for the medical student in his preclinical years is usually that of basic sciences (this is true even for those medical schools where teaching in basic sciences and clinical education is integrated). It may seem reasonable to combine studies of basic sciences with philosophy of science and logic to form a scientific attitude to basic science as well as a foundation for the clinical years to follow.

During the clinical years, the teaching of clinical research as exemplified by controlled clinical trials, cohort studies, etc., should be accompanied by courses in statistics and courses in the foundation of ethical reasoning. This should then be followed by clinical decision making and continued seminars on specific ethical issues as an integrated part of the clinical education.

As to the question: 'Who should teach', one may remember that ethics is a branch of philosophy and the competence is usually to be found within the faculty of philosophy or humanities. Nevertheless criticism has been raised against non-medical teachers for being too theoretical, for their teaching tradition being alien to medical teaching and with poor roots in the specific nature of medical ethical problems. The question raised is: Is a non-physician theorist/observer not as good a teacher as a clinical (physician) ethicist/participant? or to put it differently: Is knowledge changed when it is applied? Mark Siegler (1981) who discusses this refers to Soren Kierkegaard who answers these questions in the following way:

Let us imagine a pilot, and assume that he has passed every examination with distinction, but that he has not as yet been at sea. Imagine him in a storm; he knows everything he ought to do, but he has not known before how terror grips the seafarer when the stars are lost in the blackness of night; he has not known the sense of impotence that comes when the pilot sees the wheel in his hand become a plaything for the waves; he has not known how the blood rushes into the head when one tries to make calculations at such a moment; in short, he has had no conception of the change that takes place in the knower when he has to apply his knowledge (Oden 1978).

Experience from the teaching of statistics has for many physicians underlined clinical experience as a prerequisite for effective teaching and many medical students who have attended courses in decision making and statistics led by professional theorists have only become more confused.

A multi-disciplinary approach therefore seems important. The extension of our question is therefore: Who should be responsible for education in medical decision making, ethics and health economics: the faculty of medicine, philosophy, humanity, or economics? There may be no single answer to this question, but it is the author's opinion that the responsibility probably ought to rest with the faculty of medicine, which would then collaborate intensively with the other relevant faculties in producing appropriate courses and obtain the optimal integration into the clinical experiences of the student in a harmonious way.

At some universities ethics is taught concurrently with a literature course using selected reading to illuminate specific issues. Some universities have weekly seminars where ethical issues extracted from hospitalized patients in the wards are presented and discussed. Riis (1981) has pointed out that, on elucidating the size of the problem in daily clinical work, a prospective analysis of clinical decision making in a department of internal medicine was carried out and that 25 per cent of the cases represented problems which could not be solved without clinical weighting. The clinical teaching material therefore seems sufficient to form the basis of 'live education' which is given high priority by both those who teach and those who are taught.

In this connection it is worth mentioning interdisciplinary, intersectoral, or multidisciplinary approaches to teaching and research. This type of research and teaching seems more necessary than ever but it demands open-mindedness and an imaginative and flexible use of knowledge and intelligence to reach a state of transdisciplinary insights. Not all good teachers and researchers, physicians, ethicists, and health economists fulfil these criteria and the personality characteristics are in some respects more related to artistic pattern recognition than deductive logic. The success of these programmes based on interdisciplinary collaboration is therefore often very person related.

Within organized medicine, that specific issue of ethics which deals with the allocation of scarce resources is probably the most important one from a policy standpoint and also from a public health and a philosophical point of view. It is probably safe to say that the problem of distributive justice may be not only the most importunate and urgent but also one of the most difficult philosophical issues of our times. The average physician meets this problem every day. Any medical education which has not dealt with it seems inadequate. This is a field shared by the health economist and the ethicist and should be dealt with in a separate course late in the graduate education and be followed up in all postgraduate specialist education.

Postgraduate education

It is normally the case that the development of postgraduate courses precedes graduate teaching. New journals often precede textbooks in the field. *Social Science and Medicine*, the *Journal of Medical Ethics*, *Philosophy and Public Action*, the *Journal of Medicine and Philosophy*, the *Journal of Philosophy of Medicine*, and the *International Journal of Health Technology Assessment* reflect the postgraduate interest in medicine and humanity. Many institutes and centres devoted to the study of ethics and humanity have evolved. Chairs in technology assessment and humanities, bioethics, medical ethics, and health economics are being created. No major conference in medicine is taking place now without lectures or workshops devoted to ethical, health economic or technology assessment issues being included. Several countries have established postgraduate courses for senior physicians and WHO and the EEC have both acted on the issue of education in these areas. The field is developing rapidly, which may reflect a changing philosophical paradigm not only in health care but also in society at large, perhaps reflecting a Darwinistic survival mechanism of our culture in a rapidly changing technological world.

References

Oden, T. C. (ed.) (1978). *Parables of Kierkegaard*. Princeton University Press, Princeton, New Jersey. p. 38.

Riis, P. (1981). Comments. In Bankowski, Z. and Corvera Bernardelli, J. (eds.) *Medical ethics and medical education*. XIVth CIOMS Round Table Conference. CIOMS, Geneva.

Siegler, M. (1981). Comments. In Bankowski, Z. and Corvera Bernardelli, J. (eds.) *Medical ethics and medical education*. XIVth CIOMS Round (Table Conference. CIOMS, Geneva.

Wulff, H. R. (1981a) *Rational diagnosis and treatment*, 2nd edition. Blackwell Scientific, Oxford.

Wulff, H. R. (1981b) How to make the best decision. Philosophical aspects of clinical decision theory. *Medical Decision Making* **1**, 277–83.

Wulff, H. R. (1986) Rational diagnosis and treatment. *Journal of Medicine and Philosophy* **11**, 123–34.

11

Epilogue: a chairman's reflections

E. M. EPPEL

The international workshop that was based on the preceding chapters was highly economical in the sense that it was assumed that participants had read all the papers beforehand thus permitting maximum time for discussion involving the sharing of experience, and the pursuit of new and sometimes unexpected ideas arising from the main themes that had been tabled. 'Serendipity' was, in consequence, a keynote of the proceedings, and one of the objects of this epilogue is to try to reflect some of the atmosphere generated in the group by this stimulating interdisciplinary approach, and to try to pick out some dominant trends and preoccupations occurring in the discussions.

It was clear that at first many of those present manifested a mixture of interest, optimism, and scepticism: 'interest' because of the social importance and strong valencies of the issues involved, 'optimism' because of the recognition that new insights and perceptions have elsewhere been generated in 'the no man's land' between academic disciplines and established research territories, 'scepticism' because *prima facie* economics and medical ethics might seem unlikely partners for a productive alliance. Their practical connection in the world of health care could be readily, if superficially, seen; the possibility that the conceptual frameworks and analytical tools of these disparate disciplines might be applied to each other with mutual advantages seemed to some as yet another example of the triumph of hope over experience. In truth, initially, the traffic seemed to be largely a one-way flow with the economists establishing an agenda, and presenting a new and for many a rather strange framework of ideas within which to review well-established assumptions about ethical codes and behaviour in medicine. Subsequently the influences became markedly reciprocal, and all parties not only learned a good deal, but moved from defended positions to take up more accommodating stances to apparently alien notions.

In the event, 'interest' was for most deepened and extended, 'optimism' for a new, if modest, synthesis was at least maintained, and 'scepticism' while by no means (and how could it be in such a gathering?) completely banished was certainly much attenuated by cogent and flexible argument and good humour.

I have expatiated somewhat on the intellectual 'feeling tone' of the discussions based on the papers since 'outcomes' of interchanges of this kind should not be measured solely by the number of ideas committed to published documentation. The relevance of this was appreciated by the economists among others, arising from the recognition of 'process utility' as a significant element of transaction in medical practice (the economists seemed to accord it a lower value than 'outcome utility'); in the distinctions drawn between 'efficiency' as a measurable, mechanistic concept, and 'effectiveness' involving methods of attaining goals without being committed to outmoded industrial ideas about 'the one best way'. These and other comparable discussions highlighted areas where different academic and professional cultures had conditioned their members to adopt attitudes and expectations which at first they assumed were incontrovertible and/or obvious to everyone else. An encouraging product of this intensive cross-disciplinary approach was the way in which people were prepared to modify or enlarge these cultural outlooks, and at least to suspend disbelief about the conclusions reached by those starting from markedly different conceptual premises from their own.

Early in the proceedings someone asked, in effect 'What difference does the economists' view make if we adopt it, even as an hypothesis?' A consensual answer was that at the very least it forces the medical profession to think more, and more clearly about what it is producing. Throughout, both in the papers and in the discussions, the economists tried to clarify the tensions between medical ethics and economics in decision making in health care, and to analyse why they exist. They attributed these largely to the nature of health care as a 'commodity' and to the phenomenon of patients' perceptions of the uncertainties that surround it. Their claim is that medical ethics came into existence largely as a reaction to these uncertainties and as a way of regulating and ameliorating the associated problems. The 'utility of ethical codes' in this conceptualization can change to 'disutility' if they are used to dominate important issues related to 'social efficiency and social equity'. In other words if each doctor demands to pursue the best health care for each of his patients in clinical freedom, collectively this is very unlikely to add up to the greatest benefit to society, or indeed to promote a model of health care based on distributive justice. It was suggested that when doctors became involved in policy making and pronounce on relative social values they go beyond their competence, at least *qua* doctors, and that such judgements should be made by society (*sic*), or its representatives. This was strongly countered by medical and administrative participants citing formulations for involving doctors in larger decision-making groups, and practical examples of their operation.

It was widely acknowledged, however, that in the allocation of scarce resources doctors are repeatedly faced with short-run distribution problems that may run counter to consideration of larger social costs and benefits. An issue that obtrudes itself persistently is whether individual doctors should, or do, take into account aspects of these wider social costs. The economists' standpoint is that doctors usually subordinate the ethic of 'the common good' to the ethic of 'virtue and duty' which is seen by them (according to the economists) as the core of traditional medical ethics. The problem of reconciling the individual responsibility and concern embedded in the 'conventional' codes with the social implications of a putative, new 'health care ethical code' is clearly a key issue for future exploration and analysis.

Such an apparently uncompromising challenge to the effectiveness of medical ethics, or at least the economists' understanding of them, stimulated criticism of the utilitarian philosophy which underpinned the economists' case.

It was claimed from various standpoints that 'utilitarianism' had been unwittingly misused or misinterpreted, and in consequence the philosophical exegeses offered by Downie, and Matthews (discussant) enhanced the understanding of the social–ethical foundations of the Mooney–McGuire argument. The model of the market advanced by the economists came under pressure. For example it was maintained by some that the market was in fact more humane and motives involved in it more varied than the model allowed. It was also claimed that medicine is more humane than any market. On this, as in other issues, manifestations of William James's 'tough and tender minded personalities' permeated some parts of the debate. The neoclassical utilitarian brand of economics that constituted the frame of reference was, however, widely accepted, with reservations, as a valuable new starting point for the reconsideration of medical ethics. Some felt that it would be useful to be able in another context perhaps to examine the consequences of applying other modern economic theories as analytical tools.

The 'virtue and duty' image of medical ethics accepted by the economists was challenged as inadequate and misleading by some of the protagonists. It seemed to ignore the wide range of individual differences found among doctors and medical procedures even within a single society, and also the extent to which many, especially in positions of institutional responsibility, take wider social/economic/ethical factors into account both in clinical settings and in resource allocation (e.g. Gillon and Jennett).

The historical changes in the development in ethical codes were sketched by Sohl and more recent trends and influences on current ethical preoccupations analysed by ten Have—there has in recent decades been a gradual but pronounced turning away in medical ethics from traditional deontology towards new concepts involving 'systematic and continuous reflection on the norms and values guiding medical theory and praxis as part of a more encompassing health-care ethics'.

Discussion focused on the discrepancy between the ideals embodied in medical–ethical codes and actual behaviour. Even the formalizing effects of codification itself were criticized as potentially increasing the gap between ideal systems and the implementation of obligations to real patients. These reflections excited further explorations of the variations between mythology and practice in medical fields, between ideals and norms, and even between illusion and reality. It appears that the recurrence of these themes induced many, not least the economists, to enlarge and extrapolate some of their basic assumptions against the background of a developing awareness of the 'productive value of the original Mooney–McGuire thesis'.

There could be no doubt that doctors are and will be increasingly, distributors of scarce resources, and that, although personal care and face-to-face relationships will continue to characterize most clinical practice, major improvements in health will progressively depend on changes in environmental circumstances and behaviour patterns. The discussions returned frequently to consider the dictum pronounced in ten Have's paper to the effect that what is true at the level of institutional interactions may not be necessarily true for interactions between individuals. The inferences drawn seemed reasonably clear—that just as macro-resource allocation draws the boundaries for micro(interindividual)-resource allocation, so general social ethics (the preoccupation of the utilitarian economists) create the framework for medical ethics. The root problem is to keep both these categories separate conceptually and yet combine them meaningfully for practical action. Few desiderata are more compelling and challenging. Inevitably more progress was made in the clarification of the questions than in the provision of solutions, but that at least is the beginning of wisdom and a prerequisite for future development.

There was, inevitably, concentration on the use of words going beyond the examination of the denotations of special sign-languages towards genuine semantic considerations. Much of this touched on perennial issues in philosophy and social analysis, for example the motive and validity of the distinctions repeatedly made between the 'individual' and 'society'. It was considered by some that the economists' concept of rationality, in effect equating it with self-interest (whatever that might be?) was perhaps too simple and inflexible in the light of modern knowledge of cognitive processes and 'personality' generally. Indeed it was suggested that the only adequate account of 'rationality' was one that enabled the incorporation of elements of 'irrationality' of thought and impulse. The term 'autonomy', prominent especially in relation to the development of patients' rights, received much critical analysis, leading to the recognition of a more multi-dimensional understanding of its connotations. Even the notion of 'rights' (Roscam Abbing) did not escape criticism that invoked among others the memory of Jeremy Bentham. There were sharp debates on whether 'health' even if acknowledged as a 'utility' has to be conceived as an absolute or as a condition for other satisfactions—and, if the latter, what might they be? Even if they could be adequately determined, can they be compared and measured against one another? The concept of the 'quality of life' and recently developed techniques for trying to assess this roused much interest among participants.

Looming over all the discussions was the recognition of the phenomenon of 'change'—in society, in medicine, in ethical principles, in sentiments, in attitudes, and in dispositions, not to mention economic circumstances. This significant background feature of the whole proceedings was implied or exemplified in many places, for example by Hucklenbroich, Sohl, Gillon, ten Have, but such conceptual formulations of 'change' as were offered seemed relatively simple, and mainly derived from mechanical models or analogies. There were few attempts to propound any developmental approaches to changing processes in society and medicine, though Sohl, for example, reminded the conference that only in this century are we nearing the position of counting all human beings as being human. The idea of 'moral progress' (or 'moral retrogression') as reflected in the changing denotations of the terms 'neighbour' or 'person' was only rather perfunctorily dealt with—inevitable perhaps in such a brief, densely packed colloquium, but the issue once raised clearly has implications for future consideration.

The assumption of a special relationship between doctor and patient in the clinical situation was queried both in the accounts of the nature and impact of medical-expert systems (Hucklenbroich, and Pinch (discussant)) on the doctor's feeling of responsibility and autonomy, and in the issues raised (Downie, and Matthews (discussant)) about the doctor's development more as a dispenser of health care technology in a team than as an individual caring person. Jennett pointed to the circumstance that until comparatively recently doctors could do little more than diagnose and 'care' for patients. Nowadays armed with expensive techniques of investigation and potential cure they are confronted with new dilemmas about their obligations and roles in medicine and society. The cost of these technologies and the thrust of their quasi-self-generating culture require that they be funded by third parties whose presence induces new moral obligations for doctors, and for patients. It raises acutely such vital questions as the need to search for rules to regulate the switching of resources from one patient to another, or the final discontinuance of treatment in hopeless cases.

Repeatedly, the value that would accrue from the availability of comparative data on these issues was made plain. Some information was, of course, presented on the cultural and practical differences among the nations and health care services represented at the workshop, for example it was suggested by Sohl that Scandinavian countries may have a weaker concept of 'individuality' than some others, as a result of their not having had the kind of historical Renaissance that characterized other European countries. Valuable indications of variations in laws relating to medical conduct were presented by Roscam Abbing, but little was offered on practices associated with medical codes (whether explicit or implicit) among more disparate cultures. The salient issue of multi-racial societies and the variety of assumptions and expectations about ethical codes, and conflicts of interest, embodied in them received only fleeting recognition.

It was clear that there is an urgent need to develop and introduce effective systems of education in these matters for doctors and members of related professions. The main features of the case were presented by Vang, and Todd (discussant) but the problem surfaced in other parts of the discussion. It was maintained that what is needed apart from special instruction in ethics (and logic?) is a sound general education for those intending to be doctors. Sohl and others pointed to the demise of the basic classical education that most doctors had in the past (though it may be unwise to assume automatic 'transfer of training' in too many of these cases). What does seem undeniable is that a broad education leading to the extension of understanding and empathy to wider groups and the cultivation of social sensitivity are desirable for doctors working in contemporary society.

The questions of who should teach ethical principles and ethical styles of thinking? and how? and when? were raised. Perhaps the emphasis might have been placed on the who, how, and when of the 'learning' appropriate to doctors at different stages of their careers. There was consensus that, whatever of this might take place, and however effectively, at undergraduate level, it is later that the greatest impact will occur, that is, as a form of continuing education for experienced practitioners with reinforcement and 'feed-back' from their encounters with actual dilemmas, and their need to make moral choices. It was also agreed that it would be desirable to try through this education to help doctors to cope with 'uncertainty without either excessive indecision or grasping for authoritative answers'. This might be seen as a necessary keynote for all education, but is especially relevant for doctors.

It was also clear from many parts of the discussions that more input on psychological issues would have been, and would be, helpful. These related to psychological aspects of moral development in individuals and groups, to conscious and unconscious factors affecting choices, and to elements of the 'mechanisms of defence' that could influence behaviour. The economists for example specifically raised such questions as the nature of 'motives' and referred to the problem of 'internalizing' social–ethical principles. These are matters on which psychological theories and research can throw some light or at the least help to reformulate the questions productively.

Finally, it is clear that the areas of concern dealt with at this workshop—the expanding field of medical ethics examined here within a challenging economic perspective—exemplified and helped to bring into focus many of the general ethical and social dilemmas of changing, pluralistic, and sometimes confused societies. They involve consideration of the nature, sources, and legitimation of power; of decision making. New processes and new technologies in medicine demand new definitions of old axioms and presumptions, for example about life and death, about parenthood, about individuality, about human aspirations. There used to be an old game played in philosophy tutorial classes, and elsewhere. It asked people to indicate whom they would wish to save if there was room for only four out of a dozen deserving cases on a raft in a shipwreck—and to give their (moral) reasons. That game has now to be openly played in reality more and more often, and will be by more and more doctors and others in the foreseeable future.

The chapters printed here and the workshop generally tried to look at these issues from slightly oblique vantage points. It challenged some accepted notions and in so doing may have generated some intellectual unease in anyone who thought that he or she knew the answers already, or that they were easy to find. The proceedings were often most vivid and stimulating when the participants drew on their personal experiences and tried to make conceptual sense of them with the help of others. We hope that this account of what took place may stimulate readers to ask new, and even more relevant, questions and offer even more penetrating criticism.

Appendix

List of Discussants

Matti Hakama, University of Tampere, Finland.

Siv Kimbré, National Board of Health, Sweden.

Eric Matthews, University of Aberdeen, Scotland.

Gavin Mooney, University of Copenhagen, Denmark.

Trevor Pinch, University of York, England.

Alan Rowe, Vice Chairman, Central Ethical Committee, and of the Ethical Committee of the Standing Committee of Doctors of the European Community.

Frans Rutten, Rijksuniversiteit Limburg, The Netherlands.

John Todd, Sheffield Health Authority, England.

Aine Uhde, University of Bergen, Norway.

Index

157